First Printing..July 2011
Second Printing ....September 2011
Third Printing..July 2012
Fourth Printing .... June 2013
Fifth Printing... June 2014
Sixth Printing... June 2015
Seventh Printing ....June 2016
Eighth Printing..October 2016
Ninth Printing.. July 2017
Tenth Printing .... July 2018
Eleventh Printing .... July 2019
Twelfth Printing ....July 2020
Thirteenth Printing ....July 2021
Fourteenth Printing...July 2022

This is D.A. service material, produced in response to the needs of D.A. members for information and shared experience on specific service-related subjects. It reflects the guidance of the Twelve Traditions, the General Service Board (GSB), and the General Service Office (GSO), and is developed from the shared experience of D.A. members throughout the Fellowship. Since service material reflects the current and ever-developing conscience of our Fellowship as a whole, it does not undergo the usual D.A. literature approval process, which requires final approval by the World Service Conference (WSC). Instead, service material may be updated periodically under the auspices of the General Service Board to reflect current Fellowship experience.

Printed in the United States of America

Contents

Printed in the United States of America

CHAPTER 1 – PRINCIPLES OF SERVICE

A. The Twelve Steps of D.A.

Service begins with the Twelve Steps, culminating with Step Twelve, which urges us to carry this message to compulsive debtors. These principles of recovery, particularly Step Twelve, provide the foundation for Service, since it is impossible to give away what we do not have.

1. We admitted we were powerless over debt—that our lives had become unmanageable.
2. Came to believe that a Power greater than ourselves could restore us to sanity.
3. Made a decision to turn our will and our lives over to the care of God as we understood Him.
4. Made a searching and fearless moral inventory of ourselves.
5. Admitted to God, to ourselves, and to another human being the exact nature of our wrongs.
6. Were entirely ready to have God remove all these defects of character.
7. Humbly asked Him to remove our shortcomings.
8. Made a list of all persons we had harmed and became willing to make amends to them all.
9. Made direct amends to such people wherever possible, except when to do so would injure them or others.
10. Continued to take personal inventory and when we were wrong promptly admitted it.
11. Sought through prayer and meditation to improve our conscious contact with God as we understood Him, praying only for knowledge of His will for us and the power to carry that out.
12. Having had a spiritual awakening as the result of these Steps, we tried to carry this message to compulsive debtors and to practice these principles in all our affairs.

The Twelve Steps and Twelve Traditions. Copyright © A.A. World Services, Inc. Adapted and reprinted with permission.

B. The Twelve Traditions of D.A.

The Twelve Traditions begin with the idea of D.A. Unity, and it is this principle which is one of the surest guides to a proper attitude in Service. The Traditions help us to put into practice the principles we have learned from the Steps and enable us to live in harmony with our fellows.

1. Our common welfare should come first; personal recovery depends on D.A. unity.
2. For our group purpose there is but one ultimate authority, a loving God as He may express Himself in our group conscience. Our leaders are but trusted servants; they do not govern.
3. The only requirement for D.A. membership is a desire to stop incurring unsecured debt.
4. Each group should be autonomous except in matters affecting other groups or D.A. as a whole.
5. Each group has but one primary purpose—to carry its message to the debtor who still suffers.
6. A D.A. group ought never endorse, finance, or lend the D.A. name to any related facility or outside enterprise lest problems of money, property, and prestige divert us from our primary purpose.
7. Every D.A. group ought to be fully self-supporting, declining outside contributions.

8. Debtors Anonymous should remain forever nonprofessional, but our service centers may employ special workers.
9. D.A., as such, ought never be organized; but we may create service boards or committees directly responsible to those they serve.
10. Debtors Anonymous has no opinion on outside issues; hence the D.A. name ought never be drawn into public controversy.
11. Our public relations policy is based on attraction rather than promotion; we need always maintain personal anonymity at the level of press, radio, and films.
12. Anonymity is the spiritual foundation of all our Traditions, ever reminding us to place principles before personalities.

The Twelve Steps and Twelve Traditions. Copyright © A.A. World Services, Inc. Adapted and reprinted with permission.

C. The Twelve Promises of D.A.

In the program of Debtors Anonymous, we come together to share our journey in recovering from compulsive debting. There is hope. When we work D.A.'s Twelve Steps and use D.A.'s Twelve Tools, we develop new ways of living and begin to receive these gifts of the program:

1. Where once we felt despair, we will experience a newfound hope.
2. Clarity will replace vagueness. Confidence and intuition will replace confusion and chaos. We will live engaged lives, make decisions that best meet our needs, and become the people we were meant to be.
3. We will live within our means, yet our means will not define us.
4. We will begin to live a prosperous life, unencumbered by fear, worry, resentment or debt.
5. We will realize that we are enough; we will value ourselves and our contributions.
6. Isolation will give way to fellowship; faith will replace fear.
7. We will recognize that there is enough; our resources will be generous and we will share them with others and with D.A.
8. We will cease to compare ourselves to others; jealousy and envy will fade.
9. Acceptance and Gratitude will replace regret, self-pity and longing.
10. We will no longer fear the truth; we will move from hiding in denial to living in reality.
11. Honesty will guide our actions towards a rich life filled with meaning and purpose.
12. We will recognize a Power Greater than ourselves as the source of our abundance. We will ask for help and guidance and have faith that it will come.

All this and more is possible. When we work this program with integrity and to the best of our ability, one day at a time, a life of prosperity and serenity will be ours.

D. The Twelve Concepts for D.A. Service

Just as the Twelve Steps are guides for personal recovery and the Twelve Traditions are guides for group unity, the Twelve Concepts are guides for World Service. These Concepts serve as a path for Twelfth Step work on a world service level, and show how the D.A. groups, the World Service Conference, and the Debtors Anonymous General Service Board work together to carry recovery in D.A. to the still suffering debtor.

1. The ultimate responsibility and authority for Debtors Anonymous World Services should

always remain with the collective conscience of our whole Fellowship as expressed through the D.A. groups.

2. The D.A. groups have delegated complete administrative and operational authority to the General Service Board. The groups have made the Conference the voice and conscience for the whole Fellowship, excepting for any change in the Twelve Steps, Twelve Traditions, and in Article 10, the General Warranties, of the Conference Charter. [1]

3. As a traditional means of creating and maintaining a clearly defined working relationship between the groups, the World Service Conference, and the Debtors Anonymous General Service Board, it is suggested that we endow these elements of world service with a traditional "Right of Decision" in order to ensure effective leadership.

4. Throughout our Conference structure, we maintain at all levels a traditional "Right of Participation," ensuring a voting representation.

5. The traditional Rights of Appeals and Petition protect the minority opinion and ensure the consideration of personal grievances. [2]

6. The Conference acknowledges the primary administrative responsibility of the Debtors Anonymous General Service Board. [3]

7. The Conference recognizes that the Charter and the Bylaws of the Debtors Anonymous General Service Board serve as governing documents and that the Trustees have legal rights, while the rights of the Conference are spiritual, rooted in the Twelve Traditions. The Concepts are not legal instruments.

8. The Debtors Anonymous General Service Board of Trustees assumes primary leadership for larger matters of overall policy, finance, and custodial oversight, and delegates authority for routine management of the General Service Office.

9. Good leaders, together with appropriate methods for choosing them at all levels, are necessary. At the world service level, the Board of Trustees assumes primary leadership for D.A. as a whole.

10. Every D.A. service responsibility should be equal to its service authority as defined by tradition, resolution, or D.A.'s Charter.

11. While the Trustees hold final authority for D.A. World Service administration, they will be assisted by the best possible staff members and consultants. Therefore, serious care and consideration will always be given to the compensation, selection, induction to service, rotation, and assignments for special rights and duties for all staff with a proper basis for determining financial compensation.

12. The Conference of Debtors Anonymous will observe the spirit of the Traditions, taking care not to become powerful and wealthy; having sufficient operating funds with a prudent reserve; having no authority over any other members; making important decisions by discussing and voting on issues wherever possible by substantial unanimity; not acting in a punitive way; not inciting public controversy; never performing any acts of government; and finally, always remaining democratic in thought and action. [4]

The Twelve Concepts for Debtors Anonymous were inspired by the Twelve Concepts for Alcoholics Anonymous and are modified with permission of A.A. World Services, Inc.

E. Questions and Answers about Service

We perform service at every level: personal, meeting, Intergroup and World Service. Service is vital to our recovery. Only through service can we give to others what has been so generously given to us.

1   Rev. 8/2005 D.A. World Service Conference
2   Rev. 8/2006 D.A. World Service Conference
3   Rev. 8/2006 D.A. World Service Conference
4   Rev. 8/2004 D.A. World Service Conference

What Is Service?

To serve means to render assistance, be of use, or help. Service, then, means assistance to an individual or a group. We help other D.A. members by attending meetings, listening, and sharing our own experiences. We help the group by performing tasks such as chairing or leading the meeting, being treasurer, or taking notes at a business meeting. In D.A. we learn to define service as giving to others what we have so generously been given.

The primary purpose of our Fellowship is to carry the message to other compulsive debtors who still suffer, so any service, no matter how small, is important. Helping to set up and put away chairs or taking telephone calls from other D.A. members are simple ways in which we can give service right from the beginning. We are encouraged to give what we can, when we can.

Why Give Service?

For many of us, life has seemed a struggle to get and keep what we could for ourselves. We sometimes compulsively overspent or underspent in an effort to convince ourselves that we had enough. In D.A., we learned that one way to experience more abundance and prosperity in our lives was by giving of ourselves to others. This is the Twelfth Step in action. In other words, we help ourselves by offering service to fellow members and to D.A. as a whole. By doing so, we decrease our self-obsession and isolation.

When we volunteer our time to D.A., we are also helping to make sure that D.A. will be there when the still-suffering debtor reaches out for help. We remember attending our first D.A. meeting and recall with gratitude the people who welcomed us.

Because D.A. is a nonprofessional organization, it depends upon the participation of its members to thrive and grow. Each group benefits from the service of its members, and the organization benefits when groups send contributions to the General Service Office to help "carry the message to the debtor who still suffers" on a national and international level.

What Are the Benefits of Giving Service?

We sometimes hear D.A. members say, "When I got busy, I got better." The personal benefits we receive from giving service are without parallel: We feel useful. We experience a sense of accomplishment, which enhances our self-esteem. We gain a sense of oneness with others.

For many of us, the disease of compulsive debting is one of isolation. Giving service provides us with a direct connection to the Fellowship, lessening our isolation and loneliness. Learning how to speak up in a business meeting helps us to be more assertive in other parts of our lives. Service gives us a voice in a community of fellows who understand us.

Taking a service position such as Secretary, Treasurer, or General Service Representative for our meeting helps us to keep our commitment to our own recovery. Many members have said that had it not been for their service position, which required them to attend meetings, they might have stopped coming altogether.

How Is Service Related to Our Money and Our Higher Power?

As we learn to give freely of ourselves through service in D.A., our connection with our Higher Power is renewed and strengthened.

When we first came to D.A., many of us were convinced that having enough money would be the answer to our problems. We began to experience a new perspective when we gave service. We learned that as we gave of our time and talents, our Higher Power did for us what we could not do for ourselves. We realized that our needs were being met; we had more than enough.

Service to the fellowship is service to our Higher Power, to our fellows, and ultimately to ourselves. When we become willing to contribute, to give back, the God of our understanding meets us more than halfway. We begin to experience the freedom from financial insecurity that is promised in "The Big Book®" of Alcoholics Anonymous®. As our lives begin to change, we continue to give from a newfound sense of gratitude. We notice a cycle: we contribute freely with joy and without expectation, we discover that all our needs are met, and in gratitude, we are inspired to give again.

What Ways Are There to Give Service?

The opportunities for service in D.A. are many and varied. We soon learn that we carry the message by example; that is, we demonstrate our recovery by not debting one day at a time, by working the Steps to the best of our ability, and by continuing to practice the principles of the Twelve Steps and Twelve Traditions in all areas of our lives. The example of our recovery—without bragging or preaching—is what gives newcomers hope when they come to D.A. Newcomers can see what the program has done for us and what it can do for them if they are willing to follow our suggestions, work the steps, and live in recovery through the program.

Four levels of service—personal, group, Intergroup, and World—offer every member an opportunity for growth and recovery.

Personal Service

On a personal level, we give service by meeting newcomers after meetings or calling them during the week. When we have ongoing experience working the Twelve Steps with a sponsor, we are ready to sponsor others. Asking a sponsor for help is also being of service to our sponsors. They experience the benefits of sharing experience, strength, and hope. When we have abstained from incurring new unsecured debt for ninety days and have had two Pressure Relief Meetings for ourselves, we can sit on Pressure Relief Groups for other D.A. members.

Group Service

Even as newcomers, we learn that our presence is of value to everyone at the meeting. We can help by listening, reading when it is our turn, and sharing our own experience. We give service to the group by arriving early to help set up the meeting and staying late to help clean up. As we gain some time in the Fellowship, we can volunteer for a service position such as meeting chairperson, treasurer, or literature chair. Some groups have other positions, such as a secretary who takes notes at the monthly business meeting.

Most groups have suggested qualifications for holding a service position, such as having worked the Steps with a sponsor, having had two Pressure Relief Meetings, and having abstained from incurring new unsecured debt for at least 90 days.

Since each group is autonomous except in matters that affect D.A. as a whole, the group can set the qualifications and length of service for each position. Sometimes service positions are rotated every year or six months, sometimes every quarter. In some cases, if the meeting is new or small, a person may continue to hold a position until someone else volunteers to do that service. We have found that the group is best served when service positions rotate on a regular basis.

Intergroup Service

As we learn to handle responsibilities on a group level, we may become interested in working with recovering debtors from other meetings in our area. We can volunteer to be the Intergroup Representative for our meeting. An Intergroup consists of representatives from D.A. meetings in a defined area, such as a city and nearby suburbs, who meet periodically to provide services for the entire area. Intergroup Representative is often a six-month commitment; qualifications vary from group to group.

The Intergroup is usually responsible for a number of activities that support meetings in the area, such as keeping a list of current meeting times and locations, maintaining a phone recording with meeting information, purchasing literature in bulk and selling it to groups, sponsoring workshops, and perhaps maintaining a website. Intergroup service positions may include chairperson, secretary, treasurer, workshop/events coordinator, and public information chair. Some Intergroups may need a voice mail coordinator to maintain the phone service and return calls from newcomers. Large Intergroups that operate area offices to provide these services may require additional service positions, such as office manager.

World Service

On an international level, we can offer to be of service as our meeting's General Service Representative (GSR) or Intergroup Service Representative (ISR). The service commitment for both positions is usually for two or three years and includes attendance at the annual World Service Conference. By attending the annual D.A. World Service Conference, a GSR or ISR represents a meeting or Intergroup, respectively. GSRs and ISRs participate actively in determining the group conscience of the fellowship as a whole, and they give advice and direction to the General Service Board (GSB). They do the work of the various Conference Committees while attending the Conference and throughout the year.

They report to their meetings or Intergroups and act as the links between these groups and the GSB. The GSR may also represent the group at area or regional GSR meetings.

The suggested qualifications are to be actively working the Twelve Steps, to have had at least two Pressure Relief Meetings, and to have abstained from incurring new unsecured debt for at least one year.

In addition, those who gain experience as GSRs or ISRs may be nominated to serve as Trustees on D.A.'s General Service Board. The GSB is an incorporated trusteeship of up to 15 Trustees who serve one to two three-year terms. Its purpose is to oversee and guide D.A. on matters that affect D.A. as a whole, including D.A.'s finances, operation of the General Service Office, literature publication and distribution, and other essential D.A. functions. It also protects D.A.'s legal rights and executes its legal responsibilities.

What Challenges Do We Face When We Give Service?

We may think that because we have been elected to a service position, we have special power or control over the group. We may be tempted to use a service position to manipulate outcomes or force issues. We may take it personally if it seems our efforts are not appreciated, such as if we organize a workshop and few people attend. We sometimes forget that our job is to take action, to "do the footwork," but the results are in the hands of our Higher Power. The Second Tradition of Debtors Anonymous teaches us that "our leaders are but trusted servants; they do not govern." We are reminded to practice humility and avoid grandiosity, to serve.

Some of us climb onto a kind of service treadmill where we feel trapped, taking on more and more commitments, unable to say "no." We may fear that we will lose power and control or that the work will not get done. Many of us have learned that the work gets done in God's time, not ours. By letting go of our fears, we allow others the opportunity to enhance their own recovery by being of service.

Service may bring us a great deal of attention. Like debting and spending, it can be addictive for some of us. Eventually we have found balance through practice and prayer. We have discovered that our Higher Power is the source of our self-esteem, which is enhanced, but not dependent upon, our service work in D.A.

Some learn through painful experience the wisdom of our First Tradition, which states, "Our common welfare should come first; personal recovery depends upon D.A. unity." If we bulldoze our agenda through a business meeting, it usually results in alienating members and creating resentment in ourselves. Gradually, we have come to understand that our personal recovery—our very survival—depends on group unity. We have discovered that when we rely on the authority of a Higher Power as expressed in our group conscience, the needs of the group, and ultimately our own, are met.

We trust in our Higher Power to guide us as we become willing to use the tool of service as an integral part of our recovery. With our connection to our Higher Power firmly in place, the rewards of giving service are truly beyond measure. As we give freely of ourselves with no expectation of return, we experience increased freedom and serenity. Every contribution we make with an open heart is another step in the right direction. No contribution is too small if given freely with love.

Reprinted from the discontinued pamphlet "Service." Copyright © 2001 Debtors Anonymous General Service Board, Inc.

F. Rotation of Service Positions

The idea of rotation of service positions is one of long standing in Twelve Step fellowships. It traces its origin to the original, "long form" version of the Twelve Traditions, as originally printed by Alcoholics Anonymous® in 1946. There, the Ninth Tradition states in part: [5]

Each A.A. group needs the least possible organization. Rotating leadership is the best.

The cofounder of A.A., Bill W., also referred to the idea of rotation in A.A.'s Concept XII, which reads in part: [6]

Therefore the composition of these underlying committees and service boards, the personal qualifications of their members, the manner of their induction into service, the systems of their rotation ... will always be matters for serious care and concern.

The reasons for adoption of this idea in Twelve Step programs are obvious. As has frequently been noted, D.A. members, like those of other programs, are often ego-driven personalities. We tend to seek to dominate and control, either overtly or covertly. There is a strong drive to seek to politicize and manipulate. While these tendencies can lead to progress and positive change, they can also lead to rigidity and inflexibility. At the extreme, they can lead to division and hostility as those who are dominated or manipulated realize what is happening. Ultimately, these tendencies are anti-democratic in nature and can work to undermine the effectiveness of the D.A. Program.

Long-time service without rotation can lead to complacency and immobility. There can be a resistance to new ideas and a sense that nothing should be changed. While the phrase, "If it ain't broke, don't fix it," has some validity, all too often it is used as an excuse for inaction by those in long-term power.

On the other hand, there is a tendency on the part of many who have held positions of trust for a long time to forget that they are servants, not masters. They are the "bleeding deacons" who combine and conspire to seek to retain and expand their areas of control. Having learned to enjoy the taste of authority, they are reluctant to surrender it. They may have great passions and idealistic goals, but they increasingly tend to rely on the most political and divisive tactics to

5   Alcoholics Anonymous World Services, Inc., Alcoholics Anonymous (4th Ed. 2001) pg 565. Reproduced with permission.

6   Bill W., A.A. Service Manual Combined with Twelve Concepts for World Service, (2008-2009 Ed., Alcoholics Anonymous World Services, Inc.) pg 48. Reproduced with permission.

achieve those goals. All too frequently, these individuals forget what is good for all in the drive to achieve their personal, predetermined aims.

Because of these facts of D.A. life, it has long been the practice to limit the time anyone may serve in a given position. The importance of this practice increases with the level of responsibility and delegated authority a person may have. Thus, GSB Trustees, like Delegates, are limited to two three-year terms. However, we go further to suggest that, once having served as Trustee, a person should refrain from any similar-level position in D.A. In its Bylaws, the GSB has codified this position to prevent any former Trustee from returning to the Board or serving as an Appointed Committee Member and has urged former Trustees to avoid serving as Delegates.

The Conference has also followed this practice by urging Delegate members to serve only two three-year terms. Additionally, the Conference has recommended that a Delegate serve no more than three consecutive years on any one committee.

It should be remembered that these limits imposed by the idea of rotation leave open many possible avenues of Twelfth Step service to the member who has reached these limits. The former Delegate may always apply to become a Trustee or ACM, or Project Contributor and the former Trustee may always return to group or Intergroup service where their valuable experience may provide guidance and assistance to those first starting out in service. The opportunities for service as sponsors or PRG members should also not be overlooked. Those with knowledge and experience in D.A. recovery need not forget the helping hand that was held out to them by retreating into silence or apathy.

G. Understanding Anonymity

Anonymity as a Spiritual Principle

Anonymity is the spiritual foundation of all our traditions, ever reminding us to place principles before personalities.

—Twelfth Tradition of Debtors Anonymous

Anonymity is an important principle in the Debtors Anonymous program of recovery; it takes on different meanings depending on the circumstances. On a personal level, anonymity means that D.A. members do not reveal the names of anyone we see at meetings nor what is shared at meetings. This safeguard protects all members from identification as compulsive debtors and provides the assurance that what we share is not repeated. This is very important for all of us, and is usually a newcomer's special concern.

On the media level, anonymity means we do not disclose our membership in D.A. in the press, TV, film, or any other media. On this level, anonymity promotes the equality of all members in the Fellowship and helps to further develop the humility that is so important to our recovery.

As a spiritual principle, anonymity is part of the practice of humility and gratitude. "Principles before personalities" is a statement of our willingness to trust that we are equal and that our Higher Power speaks through all of us, without judgment. No one person speaks as an authority on the program. No position in society exemplifies spiritual principles better than others.

Personal Anonymity

Most compulsive debtors are ashamed of the circumstances of their life when they arrive at D.A. Newcomers may be fearful that others will find out about their problems. Most of us kept money problems and feelings to ourselves before joining D.A. However, our program suggests that sharing our secrets helps us to change destructive patterns in our lives. Confidentiality, one aspect of anonymity, is important because it makes sharing about our problems easier.

Without such protection, many debtors might avoid attending meetings or sharing at meetings.

Because meetings are a key tool in our recovery, they need to be a safe haven for all of us. D.A. suggests that members use only their first names at meetings and respect the anonymity of other members. This does not mean, however, that we always hide our last names from other members. At times, we may choose to reveal our last name.

Revealing Your D.A. Membership

Individual members may reveal their D.A. affiliation with friends and families. When we disclose our membership to others, some of us find it helpful to let them know that the information is something that we would prefer to share only with the people we choose. We also inform them that no revelation of our membership is to be made on the media level.

The D.A. Program is a program of attraction, and many new members come to a meeting because they met a member and liked what the member said or did. Therefore, many of us believe that when we meet someone who is looking for help, it is appropriate to reveal our D.A. membership. However, this is an entirely personal matter. When we have doubts we consult with friends or a sponsor about making such decisions.

Respecting the Personal Anonymity of Others

On a personal level, anonymity means that if we see people in meetings whom we know as friends, acquaintances or public figures, we do not reveal it to anyone. These people are in the meeting for the same reason we are. We respect their right to remain anonymous and expect the same in return.

Anonymity applies as much to the things shared as it does to the person sharing. Therefore, in addition to respecting an individual's need to keep their identity anonymous, we do not reveal the substance of what they share. Also, when we leave the meeting, we avoid gossip and criticism of one another.

Anonymity at the Media Level

> We practice anonymity, which allows us freedom of expression by assuring us that what we say at meetings or to other D.A. members at any time will not be repeated."
> —*Fourth Tool of Debtors Anonymous*

Since its beginning in 1976, the story of D.A. has appeared in newspapers and magazines and on television. These are very effective ways of carrying the message to others, and membership has always increased after a story appears. D.A. suggests that when talking with the media, anonymity is preserved by only revealing first names and never having photos or pictures published or broadcast. It is the responsibility of the individual members, not the media, to maintain this tradition.

Many D.A. members have spoken to the media and have been quoted in articles. At those times D.A. stresses caution be taken to preserve the individual's anonymity. For example, at one meeting a local news team showed up at the meeting site right before the meeting began and asked if they could tape the meeting. Of course, this would not be in accordance with the tradition of anonymity at the media level and the camera crew was sent away. However, later arrangements were made with the same television station to tape a meeting of people who volunteered to participate with the promise that their faces would not be revealed and their last names would not be used. This is an acceptable way to provide the public with information about the program without undermining the tradition of anonymity.

It is the D.A. organization that we wish to make known, not its individual members. Anonymity at the level of press, radio, TV and film deters members from speaking out as the purported voice of D.A. or capitalizing on their D.A. membership. D.A. members adhere to the tradition of anonymity because in our experience, and in the experience of other twelve-step programs, anonymity helps the fellowship flourish.

Anonymity Statement (to be used at meetings open to the public)

Some of you may be unaware of D.A.'s Eleventh Tradition, which provides that: "Our public relations policy is based on attraction rather than promotion; we need always maintain personal anonymity at the level of press, radio, and films."

As in other twelve-step fellowships, the original wording "press, radio and films" is clearly understood to include all other forms of public media that have since evolved, including television, the Internet, and social networking sites, as well as public media that may be invented in the future.

Consequently, we request that you respect this principle of anonymity whenever you tape, photograph, or broadcast reports of our meetings. There should be no television or other broadcast appearances in which the D.A. member is recognizable by appearance or voice. This also applies to any other media technology such social media or the Internet. In all media, please refer to our members by using only first names and last initials and please understand that an individual's opinion and experience in recovery is not necessarily the view of Debtors Anonymous as a whole.

Making the decision to join our Fellowship is never an easy one. If potential members saw a current member identified in the media by the use of full name or likeness, we believe this would make them less likely to seek help from D.A., and if just one person were so deterred we would consider that a tragedy for that person and all those whose lives are affected by their compulsive debting behavior. Please help D.A. keep our treasured Twelfth Tradition: "Anonymity is the spiritual foundation of all our traditions, ever reminding us to place principles before personalities."

Anonymity and the Internet

The GSB has discussed the use of web-based affinity groups by D.A. institutions on a couple of occasions in recent years. It has issued warnings to the Fellowship at large that use of these advertising-based groups can 1) result in anonymity breaks and 2) expose members to credit card advertising and other inappropriate commercialism.

Some years ago, the GSB decided never to use these ad-based services for our own internal communication, or for our communication with the Fellowship. Instead the Board pays for a professional service to disseminate the eNews, and other services for document storage.

The choice by any committee of the Conference or registered D.A. group to use ad-based services is protected by the Fourth Tradition, which suggests that all groups are autonomous. However, this Tradition also suggests that groups consider the effects of their actions on D.A. as a whole. The GSB hopes that, as an example for the newcomer, any group or committee's attempt to reach a group conscience also consider the spirit of Tradition Six, which suggests non-affiliation for the common good of the Fellowship.

On "The Traditions and Social Media"

Our Eleventh Tradition states, "...we need always maintain personal anonymity at the level of press, radio and films." This implies all forms of public media – including social media. Our Twelfth Tradition states, "Anonymity is the spiritual foundation of all our Traditions, ever reminding us to place principles before personalities." Anonymity provides protection for all members from identification as a debtor – an important safeguard, especially for newcomers.

The growing popularity of social media brings with it the increasing need for us to maintain personal anonymity. When using a Web site or any social media platform where D.A. members and non-D.A.s mingle, we should be aware that it is a form of public media. If we reveal our membership in D.A., along with our full name and/or a likeness such as a photograph, this would be in conflict with the spirit of the Eleventh and Twelfth Traditions.

[Above statement adopted by The D.A. General Service Board in 2011.]

H. Statement of Purpose of Debtors Anonymous

In D.A., our purpose is threefold: to stop incurring unsecured debt, to share our experience with the newcomer, and to reach out to other debtors.

CHAPTER 2 – SERVICE ON THE GROUP LEVEL

A. History of D.A.

The idea that would give rise to the Fellowship of Debtors Anonymous started in 1968, when a core group of recovering members of Alcoholics Anonymous® began discussing the problems they were experiencing with money. Led by a man named John H., they began an eight-year spiritual odyssey to understand the causes and conditions behind their self-destructive behavior with money.

Having little idea of how to approach this, they focused in turn on their diverse symptoms, including many different patterns of spending, saving, shopping, and earning. They first called themselves the "Penny Pinchers," and attempted to control through will power the amount of money they spent. Later, the group renamed itself the "Capital Builders," convinced that their financial problems stemmed from an inability to save money. They tried to cure this by making daily deposits into savings accounts, but this, too, failed to resolve their problems.

For the next few years, the ever-changing group of people around John H. tried addressing all of the symptoms they were suffering from but continued to fail. In addition to A.A., they attended meetings of Gamblers Anonymous, Al-Anon, and other twelve-step fellowships, hoping to find a definitive answer. Finally, as more years passed, they began to understand that their monetary problems did not stem from an inability to save or control the amount they spent or earned, but rather from the inability to stop incurring unsecured debt.

By 1971, the essence of the D.A. Program unfolded in the discovery and understanding that the act of debting itself was the threshold of the disease, and the only solution was to use the 12 Steps of Alcoholics Anonymous® to stop incurring unsecured debt one day at a time, to stay stopped, and to help others to do so. After two years, the group of recovering A.A. members disbanded. Meetings came and went, with John H. attempting desperately to hold the small and ever-changing group of financially troubled alcoholics together.

D.A. re-emerged in April 1976 when John H. and another debtor met at St. Stephen's Rectory in New York City for the first regularly scheduled D.A. meeting. Within a year, a second meeting was organized, with members outside of A.A. for the first time. By early 1982, there were five meetings in existence in the world, all of them in Manhattan.

In March 1982, representatives from those five meetings took a daring step. With many of them having been inspired by their service experience in A.A., they established a Pro tempore Board of Trustees for D.A. The Pro tem Board of five scheduled an Annual Meeting of Debtors Anonymous, held in New York City in September 1982. A permanent General Service Board for the Fellowship was created at that meeting and has existed ever since. Newly established meetings in Boston and Washington also elected Regional Trustees, and these were later joined by a Regional Trustee from Los Angeles.

D.A. remained mostly New York based during the mid-1980s, and four more Annual Meetings were held from 1983-1986, all in Manhattan. The General Service Board during this era attempted to build a service structure for the fledgling Fellowship largely on the model of A.A., but with some differences to accommodate D.A.'s much smaller size. Class B (non-debtor) trustees were added to the GSB, and the Regional Trustees were replaced by a board composed entirely of trustees to be drawn from throughout the world, in the interests of D.A. unity.

In 1987, the GSB further followed the A.A. model by creating a World Service Conference and turning to it for guidance and direction for D.A.'s future. In a bid to create a truly broad-based Fellowship, the Conference met only the first year in New York, and in subsequent years in Los Angeles, Boston, Chicago, San Francisco, and many other cities.

The biggest challenges in D.A.'s first fifteen years were the development of a service structure, the writing and adoption of a common literature, the overcoming of regional differences, and the forging of D.A. unity. In 1994, the growing importance of Intergroups was recognized when Intergroup Service Representatives joined General Service Representatives and Trustees as delegates to the annual World Service Conference.

Like most new organizations, D.A. struggled financially in its early years. On several occasions, its financial position has been perilous. Initially, volunteers fielded requests for information about D.A. A General Service Office was established in 1985 and was open a few hours a week for many years. D.A.'s original Office was located in New York but moved to the Boston area shortly before its first full-time employee was hired in 2001.

As of 2010, Debtors Anonymous had more than 500 registered meetings in more than 15 countries worldwide. It had a recovery book, a large stock of literature, and recently produced its first non-English language literature.

B. How to Start and Register a D.A. Group

1. Secure a Meeting Place

A D.A. group starts with its members. Once you have found other people interested in forming a group, the first step is to secure a meeting place. Sometimes, in the beginning, this will be at the home of one of the members of the group. However, most groups have found it more convenient to hold their meetings at a location open to the public. If the meeting continues to be held in a private home for any length of time, the group runs the risk of becoming dependent upon the individual providing the space. Usually, a local library, church, school, or community center will be willing to make space available at a reasonable rental. Since every D.A. group should be self-supporting through the contributions of its members, care should be taken to ensure that the rental is within the means of the group. Experience has shown that a clean, well-lighted location is best; it is important that it be welcoming and comfortable for newcomers.

Some groups find that the church or other facility providing space may require that the group provide insurance coverage to protect against liability. Sometimes this can be satisfied by having the group include in its rental a sum that covers the cost of an insurance rider for the host. Insurance can be found for nonprofit organizations such as a local group, but it may take some searching. Since these questions vary drastically from location to location, neither D.A. nor its GSO can provide more detailed information on this matter.

If there is enough money available, the group might want to spend a small amount to provide coffee, tea, and/or other refreshments. When this is possible, fellowship is enhanced, and newcomers may be made to feel welcome. However, it is important to be sure that the group does not spend too much on these items, neglecting its responsibility to help carry the message through contributions to GSO and Intergroups. Here, the group should develop an effective spending plan. It is also important that the group exercise great care in complying with all housekeeping requirements that the host organization may impose. A failure to leave a meeting place clean, or to comply with smoking requirements, may result in loss of the meeting space and injury to the reputation of the group, other groups, and D.A. as a whole.

2. Election of Officers

While D.A., as such, is not organized, every group needs to select officers to help carry out the primary purpose of the group. Someone must be available to open the meeting place, to make the coffee, to clean up after the meeting, and to chair the meeting itself. Someone must be selected to serve as Treasurer to hold the group's money and to pay bills. This may be done by an elected

Chair/Secretary[1], with the assistance of other members. A Chair/Secretary may also keep track of announcements, receive and send mail for the group, and ensure that the group has sufficient literature to help carry the message of D.A. recovery. The Chair/Secretary is also responsible for maintaining group records and registering the group with D.A.'s GSO (although this function may also be performed by the GSR). It is also important for the group to select a GSR who is responsible for maintaining contact between the group and D.A. as a whole. The duties of these officers are discussed in more detail later in this Manual.

3. Register your meeting annually online at www.debtorsanonymous.org/register

Members without Internet access can email office@debtorsanonymous.org to request a hard copy of the meeting registration form.

Annual registration will ensure that your meeting will be listed as active and qualifies the meeting for special votes. Meeting contacts will be automatically subscribed to eNews—the D.A. newsletter (and can unsubscribe any time via the link at the bottom of each email).

Meeting registration requires at least one point person who will provide personal information that will be kept confidential unless otherwise noted. All meetings agree to adhere to the Twelve Traditions of Debtors Anonymous. The General Service Office and the General Service Board reserve the right to approve meetings for inclusion in the D.A. website meeting directory. Criteria include that the meeting adheres to the Twelve Traditions, does not include information about outside 12-step programs or materials, and that all members are welcome. Special interest meetings (such as women or men's only meetings) are allowed to be listed in the meeting directory but they must agree to either have a password required for entrance so they may direct any member who does not meet the special meeting criteria to other meetings, or to have a contingency plan to meet one-on-one or in a small group with any member(s) who arrives at a meeting and does not meet the special meeting criteria. This in order to always carry the message, our primary purpose.

C. Sample Meeting Formats

This section contains suggested guidelines for the format of a D.A. meeting, a D.A. Newcomer First Step Meeting, and a B.D.A. meeting.

1. D.A. Meeting Format

This section contains suggested guidelines for the format of a D.A. meeting. The format may vary, depending upon the group conscience of its members, using D.A.'s Fourth Tradition as a guide. The Fourth Tradition states that "each group should be autonomous except in matters affecting other groups or D.A. as a whole," and therefore this format is suggestive only.

Opening

Usually the Chairperson or Secretary starts the meeting, welcomes everyone and then starts the introductions by saying:

"Hello. My name is _____ (first name only) and I am a compulsive debtor. Welcome to the _____(name of group) Meeting of Debtors Anonymous."

Many groups choose to open their meetings with a prayer, such as the Serenity Prayer or with a few moments of silent meditation.

Serenity Prayer

"God, grant me the serenity to accept the things I cannot change, courage to change the things I can, and wisdom to know the difference."

---

[1]   The use of the terms Chair or Secretary varies with region. The editors have chosen to conjoin these terms when referring to a trusted servant who heads up the group. Obviously, each of the tasks mentioned could be assigned to a different individual to spread the opportunities for service around the group.

Welcome Statement

"Debtors Anonymous offers hope for people whose use of unsecured debt causes problems and suffering. We come to learn that compulsive debting is a spiritual problem with a spiritual solution, and we find relief by working the D.A. recovery program based on the Twelve-Step principles.

The only requirement for membership is a desire to stop incurring unsecured debt. Even if members are not in debt, they are welcome in D.A. Our Fellowship is supported solely through contributions made by members; there are no dues or fees.

Debtors Anonymous is not affiliated with any financial, legal, political, or religious entities, and we avoid controversy by not discussing outside issues. By sharing our experience, strength, and hope, and by carrying the message to those who still suffer, we find joy, clarity, and serenity as we recover together."

Your meeting may consider reading the D.A. Inclusivity statement:

Inclusivity Statement

"Whatever your story, you are welcome in Debtors Anonymous. In D.A., we celebrate the rich, diverse experiences of people of all identities. We embrace members of any race, ethnicity, nationality, gender, sexual orientation, age, physical or mental ability, socio-economic status, religious, spiritual, or philosophical expression, or any other trait. Our various experiences benefit our recovery, so we encourage all members to value differences and actively participate in making D.A. an inclusive fellowship. Together, we create accessible and welcoming spaces for anyone with the desire to stop incurring unsecured debt, so that we may all recover one day at a time."

Some groups pass around the Twelve Steps and Tools of Debtors Anonymous for reading by group members. After the readings, announcements of any special rules, such as no smoking or eating, will often be made.

At this point, groups will ask newcomers and out-of-towners to introduce themselves (by first name only) so that they can be especially welcomed.

The Chairperson or Secretary will read "A Word to Newcomers."

A Word to Newcomers

"If you are having problems with money and debt and think you may be a compulsive debtor, you have come to the right place. Debtors Anonymous can help you. We offer face-to-face, telephone, and internet meetings, and we suggest attending at least six meetings to have an opportunity to identify with the speakers and become familiar with D.A. before deciding whether or not this program is for you. If you identify with some or all aspects of compulsive debting, we hope you will join us on the path of recovery and find the joy, clarity, and serenity that we have found in Debtors Anonymous."

Sometimes a meeting focuses specifically on the issues of a beginner in the D.A. Program. Although the format for such a meeting can vary, we find it helpful to expose newcomers to the Tools of the D.A. Program. Often, the Chairperson encourages beginners to ask questions or explain why they came to D.A.

Speaker

At this point, the speaker is introduced and asked to share their experience, strength, and hope with the group. This usually involves explaining what happened before the speaker came to D.A., how the speaker found D.A., and what their life has been like since coming to D.A.

The length of the speaker's sharing depends on the meeting format. At designated speaker meetings, the speaker may have a half hour or more, while at discussion meetings, he or she may have perhaps ten or fifteen minutes. Some meetings also impose a requirement that the speaker has not incurred any new unsecured debt for a set period of time.

Sharing

At discussion or topic meetings, when the speaker is finished, the meeting is then open for sharing from the group.

While sharing is generally by show of hands, other practices include the round robin (going around the room) or tag or pitch (each person calling on another when finished).

In some groups, the speaker may respond to someone sharing from the group. However, in D.A. we do not engage in crosstalk (members interrupting or directly addressing another sharer).

In some speaker meetings, sharing by the speaker is followed by a question and answer period.

Announcements

Announcements from the meeting's trusted servants and participating members can be made at any time during or after the sharing depending on the group conscience and the timing of the meeting.

The Literature Chairperson will announce the availability of meeting lists and literature, which some groups offer free to newcomers.

The Chairperson or Secretary encourages newcomers to speak to other members and exchange phone numbers before leaving the meeting.

Some groups ask if any members are celebrating an anniversary in D.A. or other special occasion such as 90 days of not incurring unsecured debt. In addition, some groups encourage beginners to count and share their day count until 90 days are reached.

Seventh Tradition

"D.A. has no dues or fees. We are self-supporting through our own contributions, so we pass the basket. Please give as generously as you can. However, if you cannot, please keep coming back. Keep in mind that our group's monthly expenses are $_____ (i.e., rent, literature, prudent reserve, etc.). In addition, D.A. has a service structure which depends on contributions from our group. After our group's needs are met, the suggested contribution is 45% to the General Service Office, 45% to Intergroup and 10% to the GSR Area Group. The General Service Office expenses include staff, rent for the office, administration, website upgrades and maintenance, new literature, and literature translations. Please help us meet our responsibility for supporting the Fellowship as a whole."

The D.A. General Service Board Treasurer's Report can be viewed anytime in *the DA Focus* at www.debtorsanonymous.org

Closing Statement

The Chairperson or Secretary of the meeting will normally thank the speaker and then read the Closing Statement.

CLOSING STATEMENT

"In closing, we would like to remind you that in Debtors Anonymous we practice Tradition Twelve, which is the principle of anonymity. This assures us the freedom to express ourselves at meetings and in private conversations without fear that our comments will be repeated. We keep what is shared at meetings confidential. As we work the Steps and practice D.A.'s Traditions and

Concepts, we are reminded that recovery is possible and that we are all here for a common purpose – to recover from compulsive debting one day at a time."

Many meetings close with group members joining hands and saying a prayer.

2. D.A. Newcomer's First Step Meeting Format

This page contains suggested guidelines for the format of a D.A. meeting focusing on newcomers. Depending upon the group conscience of its members, groups have autonomy to change the format to fit their needs, using D.A.'s Fourth Tradition as a guide.

Notes:

This format can be adapted for a Newcomer Breakout Meeting, in which selected meeting members hold a meeting with newcomers in a separate room. Breakout meetings typically happen before group sharing during a regular D.A. or BDA meeting.

Trusted servant is to read the italicized sentences in quotes.

Opening

Usually a Trusted Servant volunteers to lead the meeting, welcoming everyone and providing an introduction by saying:

"Hello. My name is _____" (first name only) *"and I am a debtor. Let's open the meeting with the Serenity Prayer."*

Serenity Prayer

Many groups choose to open their meetings with a prayer, such as the Serenity Prayer or with a few moments of silent meditation.

"God grant me the serenity to accept the things I cannot change, courage to change the things I can, and wisdom to know the difference."

Welcome

"Welcome to Debtors Anonymous. Debtors Anonymous offers hope for people whose use of unsecured debt causes problems and suffering. We come to learn that compulsive debting is a spiritual problem with a spiritual solution, and we find relief by working the D.A. recovery program based on the Twelve-Step principles.

The only requirement for membership is a desire to stop incurring unsecured debt. Even if members are not in debt, they are welcome in D.A. Our Fellowship is supported solely through contributions made by members; there are no dues or fees.

Debtors Anonymous is not affiliated with any financial, legal, political, or religious entities, and we avoid controversy by not discussing outside issues. By sharing our experience, strength, and hope, and by carrying the message to those who still suffer, we find joy, clarity, and serenity as we recover together."

This is the _____" (name of group) *"Newcomers First Step Meeting of Debtors Anonymous. We're glad you're here. Our goal today is to give you a few basic pieces of information about the D.A. program, share a little of our own experience with Step One, and give each of you a chance, if you would like, to tell us what brings you here today. This meeting will end after one hour; however, members are typically available for fellowship after the meeting to answer any questions you may have."*

Your meeting may consider reading the D.A. Inclusivity statement:

Inclusivity Statement

"Whatever your story, you are welcome in Debtors Anonymous. In D.A., we celebrate the rich, diverse experiences of people of all identities. We embrace members of any race, ethnicity,

nationality, gender, sexual orientation, age, physical or mental ability, socio-economic status, religious, spiritual, or philosophical expression, or any other trait. Our various experiences benefit our recovery, so we encourage all members to value differences and actively participate in making D.A. an inclusive fellowship. Together, we create accessible and welcoming spaces for anyone with the desire to stop incurring unsecured debt, so that we may all recover one day at a time."

Readings

Statement of Purpose

"In D.A., our purpose is threefold: to stop incurring unsecured debt, to share our experience with the newcomer, and to reach out to other debtors."

"Would someone like to read the Word to Newcomers?"

"Thank you. Would someone like to read the 12 Signs of Compulsive Debting?"

"Thank you. Would someone like to read the 12 Steps of D.A.?"

"Thank you. Would someone like to read the Tradition of the month and share for 1 minute on your experience with this Tradition?" (Each month, a new Tradition is discussed.)

"Thank you. Would someone like to read the Tool of the month and share for 1 minute on your experience with this Tool?" (Each month, a new Tool is discussed.)

"Thank you."

After the readings, announcements of any special rules, such as no smoking or eating, will often be made.

Introductions

"We will now go around the room and introduce ourselves by first name only. My name is _____ and I am a debtor."

We Care Sheet (optional)

Some meetings pass a We Care Sheet to help newcomers find support, including contact info for sponsors and members who are available for program calls. At the end of this document is a copy of a We Care Sheet that can be photo-copied.

"We are now going to pass around a We Care Sheet.

The We Care Sheet will circulate twice. The first time around, please check the services you need or can offer. Upon receiving the We Care Sheet a second time, please copy contact information for people that meet your needs.

The list will be destroyed at the end of the meeting to protect your anonymity.

Suggested Service Requirements: Service as a Pressure Relief Meeting (PRM) member or Sponsor recommended 90 days solvency and two Pressure Relief Meetings (PRMs). Solvency is described as not incurring new unsecured debt."

We Care Sheet

First Name	Phone/Email	Need				Can Give				Notes
		Calls/Bookends	Action Partner	Pressure Relief	Sponsor	Calls/Bookends	Action Partner	Pressure Relief	Sponsor	

Seventh Tradition

"We will now pass the basket in honor of the Seventh Tradition which states that, 'Every D.A. group ought to be fully self-supporting, declining outside contributions.' However, do not let a

lack of funds discourage you from attending this meeting, as the Third Tradition states, 'The only requirement for membership is a desire to stop incurring unsecured debt.'

"In addition, D.A. has a service structure which depends on contributions from our group. After our group's needs are met, we contribute the balance, 45% to the General Service Office, 45% to Intergroup and 10% to the GSR Area Group. Please help us meet our responsibility for supporting the Fellowship as a whole. You can donate directly to the General Service Office at debtorsanonymous.org/donate."

Solvency Count (optional)

"We will now do a solvency count. Can everyone please stand (or raise your hand) to celebrate your solvency in this program. Solvency refers to the length of time since a person last incurred new unsecured debt. Stay standing if you haven't debted in 24 hours," (applause) "30 days, 60 days, 90 days, 1 year, 2 years, 3 years, 4 years, etc."

Note: This continues until the last person sits down; there is applause after each count.

Speaker (suggested requirement for speakers: 90 days solvency and 2 PRMs)

"Step One of D.A. states that 'We admitted we were powerless over debt, that our lives had become unmanageable.'

"Our speaker, _____, will now share on Step One (suggested 10 minutes).

"Reminder that in this meeting, we focus on the solution and are committed to referencing only D.A. or A.A. Conference-approved literature and materials."

Sharing

"We will now go around the room and share on Step One or what brought you to the meeting today. You can either speak or pass. At this meeting, we do not engage in cross talk, which means providing feedback or commenting on what someone else has shared. We will have a timekeeper to ensure everyone has time to speak. May I have a volunteer to be timekeeper? Thank you."

Literature, Announcements and Fellowship

"Before we close, please note that literature is for sale after the meeting. If this is your first meeting, please raise your hand and I will give you a newcomer's packet.

"Does anyone have any D.A. related announcements?

"Reminder that everyone is welcome to fellowship after the meeting.

"Problems with money and debt can be overwhelming. As you come to understand the D.A. program, you will learn how to handle these problems. For now, we suggest you do three things:
1. Be willing to not debt, one day at a time.
2. Attend meetings regularly.
3. Find a sponsor (or temporary sponsor). A sponsor is a recovering debtor you can call outside the meeting who guides you through the Twelve Steps of D.A. with the help of the D.A. and B.D.A. Step Study Guides. Use the We Care Sheet to find a sponsor."

Closing

"In closing, we would like to remind you that in Debtors Anonymous we practice Tradition Twelve, which is the principle of anonymity. This assures us the freedom to express ourselves at meetings and in private conversations without fear that our comments will be repeated. We keep what is shared at meetings confidential. As we work the Steps and practice D.A.'s Traditions and Concepts, we are reminded that recovery is possible and that we are all here for a common purpose—to recover from compulsive debting one day at a time."

"We will now close the meeting with a reading of the Twelfth Tradition and the Promises of D.A.

"Will someone please volunteer to read the Twelfth Tradition?

"Thank you. Will someone please read the Twelve Promises?

"Thank you. Let's close with a moment of silence for the still suffering debtor followed by the Serenity Prayer."

3. BDA Meeting Format

This section contains suggested guidelines for the format of a BDA meeting. The format may vary, depending upon the group conscience of its members, using D.A.'s Fourth Tradition as a guide. The Fourth Tradition states that "each group should be autonomous except in matters affecting other groups or D.A. as a whole," and therefore this format is suggestive only.

Opening

Many groups choose to open their meetings with a prayer such as the Serenity Prayer or with a few moments of silent meditation.

The Serenity Prayer

"God, grant me the serenity to accept the things I cannot change, courage to change the things I can, and wisdom to know the difference."

Usually the Chairperson, Secretary, or another trusted servant starts the meeting, welcomes everyone, and then starts the introductions by saying, "Hello. My name is_____ (first name only) and I am a compulsive debtor and business owner. Welcome to the _____ (name of group) Meeting of Business Debtors Anonymous (BDA)."

Some groups ask all members to go around and introduce themselves by first name. At this point the Chairperson usually reads additional information about BDA

Welcome Statement

"Debtors Anonymous offers hope for people whose use of unsecured debt causes problems and suffering. We come to learn that compulsive debting is a spiritual problem with a spiritual solution, and we find relief by working the D.A. recovery program based on the Twelve-Step principles.

"The only requirement for membership is a desire to stop incurring unsecured debt. Even if members are not in debt, they are welcome in D.A. Our Fellowship is supported solely through contributions made by members; there are no dues or fees.

"Debtors Anonymous is not affiliated with any financial, legal, political, or religious entities, and we avoid controversy by not discussing outside issues. By sharing our experience, strength, and hope, and by carrying the message to those who still suffer, we find joy, clarity, and serenity as we recover together."

Business Debtors Anonymous (BDA) is a distinct and dynamic—but not a separate—part of D.A. created to focus on the recovery of members of the Fellowship who are business owners. Together, members of BDA support one another in applying the D.A. principles and tools when owning and running a business.

BDA is a part of Debtors Anonymous, a spiritual program based on the 12 Steps as adapted from Alcoholics Anonymous®.

Your meeting may consider reading the D.A. Inclusivity statement:

Inclusivity Statement

"Whatever your story, you are welcome in Debtors Anonymous. In D.A., we celebrate the rich, diverse experiences of people of all identities. We embrace members of any race, ethnicity, nationality, gender, sexual orientation, age, physical or mental ability, socio-economic status, religious, spiritual, or philosophical expression, or any other trait. Our various experiences benefit our recovery, so we encourage all members to value differences and actively participate in making D.A. an inclusive fellowship. Together, we create accessible and welcoming spaces for anyone with the desire to stop incurring unsecured debt, so that we may all recover one day at a time."

Readings

Some groups pass around and read aloud the D.A. Twelve Steps and Twelve Traditions. The following additional tools for Business Debtors Anonymous are read by the person who is leading, or by members:

Additional Tools for Business Debtors Anonymous

1. We keep separate professional and personal financial records and bank accounts.
2. We write annual one-year business plans with definable and accountable goals and targets.
3. We keep clean, orderly and accurate financial records, including Accounts Receivable, Accounts Payable, Cash on Hand, Inventory, Assets, and Outstanding Debts, and put all tax and bill due dates on our calendar.
4. We pay ourselves a salary including benefits, medical insurance, vacations and sick days.
5. We remain mindful that dollars spent should generate revenue and compare prices before making purchases.
6. We maintain clarity about the overhead and profit margins of every product or service we sell.
7. We pay our bills and invoice our clients promptly.
8. We put all our business agreements in writing and write our own Letters of Agreement.
9. We notice the competition but don't worry about it. We learn from our competitors and trust that it is an abundant universe with more than enough for everyone.
10. We detach from difficult personalities and poor paying clients and put principles before personalities.
11. We bookend before and after making commitments and difficult business decisions or actions.
12. We are willing to be in charge and responsible for our business. Professionals such as accountants, lawyers, and consultants who work for us are not our Higher Power.

After the readings, announcements of any special rules, such as no smoking or eating, will often be made.

Newcomers

At this point, groups will ask newcomers to the program and the meeting to introduce themselves by first name only so that they can be especially welcomed.

The Chairperson, Secretary or another trusted servant will read "Getting Started":

Getting Started

Based on experience, BDA recommends the following actions be taken toward recovery from incurring debt in business.

1. Stop incurring unsecured business debt one day at a time.
2. Attend meetings regularly.
3. Get phone numbers from other members. Call with questions and for support.
4. Get a sponsor and start working the 12 Steps. A sponsor is someone with more experience in working the 12 steps, and who has been practicing the principles of the BDA program in their personal or business life.
5. Begin keeping your numbers. Regularly record your expenses and income. It is suggested that your income and expenses covering at least one month be brought to your first Pressure Relief Group (PRG).
6. Get a Pressure Relief Group. Many of us come into the rooms of BDA with serious financial pressures from which we have had little or no relief, such as unpaid bills, creditors, and unpaid taxes. A Pressure Relief Group is comprised of two people with experience in working the Steps who can offer hope, possible options for relief, and solutions based on their experience.

Some meetings focus specifically on the issues of a newcomer in the BDA Program. Although the format for such a meeting can vary, we find it helpful to expose newcomers to the Steps and Tools of the D.A. Program.

Seventh Tradition

The Treasurer will make the following announcement in accordance with D.A.'s Seventh Tradition: *"Every D.A. group ought to be fully self-supporting, declining outside contributions."*

Announcements

Announcements from the meeting's trusted servants and participating members can be made at any time during or after the sharing, depending on the group conscience and the timing of the meeting. The Literature Chairperson will announce the availability of meeting lists and literature (which some groups offer free to newcomers.) The Secretary encourages newcomers to speak to other members and exchange phone numbers before leaving the meeting.

Some groups ask if any members are celebrating an anniversary in BDA or other special occasions (such as 90 days of not incurring unsecured debt one day at a time). In addition, some groups encourage beginners to share the number of days they have of not incurring unsecured debt, until 90 days are reached.

The Speaker

At this point the speaker is introduced and asked to share their experience, strength and hope with the group. This usually involves explaining what happened before the speaker came to BDA, how the speaker found BDA, and what it has been like since coming to BDA The length of the speaker's sharing depends on the meeting format. At designated speaker meetings, the speaker may have a half hour or more, while at discussion meetings he or she may have perhaps ten or fifteen minutes.

Sharing

At discussion or topic meetings, when the speaker is finished, the meeting is then open for sharing from the group. Sharing is generally by show of hands, and the speaker calls on people. Other practices include round robin (going around the room) or each person calling on another when finished (tag or pitch). In BDA we do not engage in crosstalk (members interrupting or directly addressing another sharer). In some speaker meetings, sharing by the speaker is followed by a question and answer period.

Closing Statement

The Chairperson or Secretary of the meeting will normally thank the speaker and then read the Closing Statement:

"In closing, we would like to remind you that in Debtors Anonymous we practice Tradition Twelve, which is the principle of anonymity. This assures us the freedom to express ourselves at meetings and in private conversations without fear that our comments will be repeated. We keep what is shared at meetings confidential. As we work the Steps and practice D.A.'s Traditions and Concepts, we are reminded that recovery is possible and that we are all here for a common purpose – to recover from compulsive debting one day at a time."

Many meetings close with a reading of the 12 Promises of D.A. followed by group members joining hands and saying a prayer.

D. Group Officers and their Duties

1. Meeting Chair/Secretary

The Meeting Chairperson/Secretary facilitates the meeting in accordance with the meeting format, as agreed upon by group conscience. (Meetings can have many different formats, such as speaker meetings, speaker/discussion meetings, Step meetings, literature/discussion meetings, topic meetings, "round robin" sharing meetings, etc.) The Meeting Chair/Secretary usually recognizes members who have raised their hands or spoken up indicating that they would like to share at the meeting. It is also the responsibility of the Meeting Chair/Secretary to ensure that there is no crosstalk at the meeting and that disruptive members are requested to comply with Tradition One; crosstalk is generally defined as interrupting or directly addressing another person or commenting on another person's share. At most meetings, the suggested requirements for service as Meeting Chair/Secretary are that the member has 90 days of not incurring unsecured debt and has had two Pressure Relief Meetings. It is helpful for the Meeting Chair/Secretary to have knowledge of the 12 Steps and 12 Traditions of Debtors Anonymous.

2. Treasurer

D.A.'s Treasurer's Manual: The Seventh Tradition in Action

Every D.A. group ought to be fully self-supporting, declining outside contributions.

    –   *Seventh Tradition of D.A.*

We will recognize that there is enough; our resources will be generous and we will share them with others and with D.A.

    –   *Seventh Promise of D.A.*

Introduction

Most D.A. groups elect a trusted servant to handle the money for the group. This person is usually called the Treasurer. The Treasurer typically is responsible for the Seventh Tradition collection at each meeting, paying the group's expenses, and making contributions on behalf of the group (per the group's conscience) to other D.A. service bodies including the local Intergroup, the General Service Office (GSO), and the General Service Representative (GSR) Area Group, if there is one.

Each group should be autonomous except in matters affecting other groups or D.A. as a whole.

— Fourth Tradition of D.A.

According to our Fourth Tradition, each D.A. group is autonomous, so the group conscience ultimately determines what the duties of the Treasurer are and how the treasury is handled. This pamphlet contains suggestions based on the experience, strength and hope of Treasurers around the world that will provide guidance both for groups and for current and future Treasurers.

Table of Contents:

Electing a Treasurer

Most groups elect a Treasurer for a set term such as six or twelve months. Many groups have recovery requirements for their Treasurer such as six months or a year of not incurring new unsecured debt and having had at least four Pressure Relief Meetings.

Some groups have co-Treasurer positions with staggered terms. This allows the duties to be shared and for the more experienced person to mentor the newer co-Treasurer.

It is important to remember that the Treasurer is a trusted servant and a guardian of the group's solvency.

Collecting Group Contributions

(Seventh Tradition: Every D.A. group ought to be fully self-supporting, declining outside contributions.)

At some point during a D.A. meeting the Treasurer or meeting leader makes the Seventh Tradition announcement. Many groups use language similar to that found in the suggested D.A. Meeting Format:

"D.A. has no dues or fees. We are self-supporting through our own contributions, so we pass the basket. Please give as generously as you can. However, if you cannot, please keep coming back."

"Keep in mind that our group's monthly expenses are $_____ (i.e., rent, literature, prudent reserve, etc.). In addition, D.A. has a service structure which depends on contributions from our group. After our group's needs are met, we contribute the balance, 45% to the General Service Office, 45% to Intergroup and 10% to the Area GSR Group. The General Service Office expenses include staff, rent for the office, administration, website upgrades and maintenance, new literature, and literature translations. Please help us meet our responsibility for supporting the

Fellowship as a whole."

The General Service Board Treasurer's annual report is included in the World Service Conference report, which is available at the D.A. website (www.debtorsanonymous.org). Additionally, quarterly financial updates are usually included in the DA Focus, also available at the website.

Recordkeeping

The Treasurer is expected to keep accurate and up-to-date records of the income and expenses for the group. In larger groups, there may be other trusted servants who assist with these tasks.

Some Treasurers have found that using a standard form to record how much is collected each week helps keep the treasury simple to manage and easy to understand. In some meetings, the Treasurer and the Secretary each keep a copy of the income and expense record which is updated weekly. In many large groups, the Treasurer serves with a Co-Treasurer or enlists another member to recount the money collected and initial the amount listed in the group's recordkeeping book.

Example of an Income and Expense Form

Date	Memo	Account	Balance
11/30/2011	Ending Balance - Nov 2011		550.00
12/7/2011	7th Tradition collection	75.00	575.00
12/7/2011	Literature Sales	25.00	600.00
12/7/2011	Rent - January 2012	(100.00)	500.00
12/7/2011	GSO donation - Nov 2011	(75.00)	425.00
12/7/2011	Intergroup donation - Nov 20111	(75.00)	350.00

Brief descriptions are used by the Treasurer in the Memo column in this example. The first two entries are donations received and literature sales (both income). The last three entries are monies paid out (expenses): rent for January of 2012 and donations made to the D.A. General Service Office and to the local Intergroup, based on the November 2011 Treasurer's Report and recommended distribution. The remaining balance includes only the Group's prudent and literature reserves.

Expense Categories and Reserves

While each group's needs are unique and its spending plan is generated using expense and income records possessed by the group, most groups with a group spending plan allocate funds to the following categories:
— Rent
— Literature Purchase
— Copies / Printing
— Postage
— Treasurer's Supplies (envelopes, pens, etc.)
— Special Events
— Prudent Reserve
— GSR Travel to the World Service Conference
— Contributions to General Service Office
— Contributions to Local Intergroup
— Contributions to GSR Area Group
— Special Contributions, such as John H. Scholarship and World Service Month

Generally, meetings keep a prudent reserve equal to three months of rent. Money can be set aside each month until the total amount is collected. Some groups keep their prudent reserve in a related but separate savings account.

In order to avoid incurring unsecured debt one day at a time, groups often choose to pay their rent monthly, always paying in advance for the following month.

Literature might be purchased from the Seventh Tradition collections; the Treasurer usually transfers such funds to the Literature person as needed. Another option is that literature can be purchased with the funds collected from selling the group's current literature. If the group is small and has no Literature position, the Treasurer may be asked to order and purchase the literature.

The largest annual expense for many groups is sending a General Service Representative to the annual World Service Conference. Some groups pass around a second basket to fund the GSR's travel. They announce each week what the goal is for that category and how much is still needed to fully fund the expenses. Other groups estimate how much money the group needs to collect each week and pass the basket around two or three times in a single meeting if the target amount for that week is not collected. (Many groups maintain their GSR fund completely separate from the meeting's general fund and Seventh Tradition.)

There may also be recurring expenses that are part of a service position, such as travel expenses for the meeting's Intergroup Representative to attend the monthly Intergroup meeting. There are also costs associated with copying local meeting lists and member phone lists.

Treasurer Pressure Relief Group and Pressure Relief Meetings

A Treasurer PRG and PRM can be effective for reviewing the group's finances on a regular basis, such as every three months. In addition to auditing the records, the meeting may uncover action items for the group such as the need to enhance the message at the group level of the Seventh Tradition and the Seventh Promise of D.A.

Some groups have used PRGs and PRMs to develop a group spending plan. Using past records, the Pressure Relief Group can usually determine the group's average income and estimated expenses and create categories which form the basis of the group's spending plan. However, a group spending plan should only be adopted and used once it has been approved in a business meeting.

Suggested Contributions

D.A. is self-supporting through our own contributions. This is true at the group level, Intergroup level, and World Service level. Group contributions help the fellowship carry the message to the debtor who still suffers and support the recovery efforts of its current membership. After a group's needs (income less expenses less reserves) are met, it is suggested in the D.A. Meeting Format and the D.A. GSR Pamphlet that groups donate the balance as follows:

45% to Intergroup   45% to the D.A. GSO   10% to GSR Area Group

If there is no local Intergroup and no GSR Area Group, it is suggested that 100% of the balance be donated to the D.A. General Service Office. In order to be received and properly recorded, checks and money orders for the General Service Office should:
7. Be made out to "DA-GSB"
8. Include the group's registration number*
9. Be mailed to: General Service Office, P.O. Box 920888, Needham, MA 02492-0009

*Groups can register online at www.debtorsanonymous.org. Groups are asked to register annually to avoid accidental removal from our online and other meeting databases.

The space below has been left blank for Treasurers to note to whom and where checks for your group's local Intergroup and GSR Area Group are to be sent.

Intergroup:

GSR Area Group:

In addition, contributions to the John H. Scholarship Fund support GSRs, whose groups need help paying their expenses for attending the World Service Conference.

There is also an annual appeal for D.A.'s World Service Month, in April of each year, as well as additional collections for literature creation and publications, and other special activities.

Safeguarding Funds

Some D.A. groups find it helpful to have a group checking and savings account. Other groups securely keep the treasury in cash and get money orders when needed. The Treasurer usually keeps the group's funds and passes them on to the next Treasurer at the end of their term.

Note: Use of personal checks in group transactions is not recommended. Instead, if cash cannot be used, group funds should be used to purchase a money order.

Opening a Group Checking Account

If a group decides to open a checking account, the members will want to consider who shall be able to sign on the account. It is recommended that the signatories meet requirements similar to those of the Treasurer position (this is, six months or a year of not incurring new unsecured debt and having had at least four Pressure Relief Meetings.) It is important for those offering to serve a term as bank signatories to understand that they may be asked by the bank to use their full names and show identification which means that they will break their anonymity. Groups have found that it is best to choose at least one member, in addition to the Treasurer, who is able to sign checks. Some groups even make it a requirement that two authorized members sign every check.

The procedures for opening a bank account differ from country to country. In the United States, a group must first request and receive an Employer Identification Number (EIN) from the Internal Revenue Service. This is done with IRS Form SS-4, which can be filled out online at www.irs.gov in about two minutes. The form may also be completed in hard copy. In Form SS-4, in Type of Entity, select "Other nonprofit organization," then enter "Social Group." In Reason for Applying, check "Banking Purpose," then enter "Open a group checking account." Note that the D.A. General Service Office has a policy not to share the EIN number of the non-profit.

Whenever a group opens a bank account it is suggested that the registered group number be included as part of the name on the account. Groups may choose not to use "Debtors Anonymous" in front of the group number to protect the anonymity of the persons signing on the account.

It is also good practice to keep bank information up to date. When a new Treasurer is elected they will need to be added as a signatory on the account and a prior signatory can be rotated off.

Disbursing Funds

The group will determine the autonomy the Treasurer is to have regardings the disbursement of funds. Some groups leave the disbursement of all funds to the Treasurer's discretion within the guidelines established by the group's spending plan. Other groups request that all disbursements, no matter how small, be approved at the monthly business meeting. Some groups identify specific line items from the spending plan or maximum amounts for reimbursement that the Treasurer may pay without group approval but require a group conscience on everything else. In either case, a record of all expenditures should be maintained.

The Treasurer will want to make sure he or she knows exactly when expenses such as rent are due and make sure that payments are all made in a regular and timely fashion to avoid incurring late charges or unsecured debt at the group level.

It is also important to remember the spiritual principle expressed in the Twelfth Concept for D.A. World Service that D.A. groups have sufficient operating funds with a prudent reserve, but not become wealthy. After the group's expenses are met including the prudent reserve, the excess should be distributed as described in the "Suggested Contributions" section.

Groups outside the United States should refer to the FAQ later in this document titled, How can groups outside the USA make contributions to the GSO and purchase literature?

Online Bill Pay

Currently, the General Service Office is able to accept online payments from U.S. members and groups who can use the Internet-based online Bill Pay service of their bank to send contributions to D.A. For members and groups that do not have Internet access, most banks allow customers to fill out Bill Pay paperwork in person at a branch office.

Arrange for online Bill Pay as follows:

The member or group should set up the "payee" as "DA-GSB" with the following address:

General Service Office
P.O. Box 920888
Needham, MA 02492-0009

If your bank's system has a memo field, include your email address there.

Once the setup has been completed, the member or group can then send funds anytime they want directly from their account.

Electronic Funds Transfer

D.A. members and groups now have the option to make an electronic funds transfer to the General Service Office. The link to the current system is found at https://debtorsanonymous.org/donate.

This service is also available to international members and groups.

Presenting the Treasurer's Report

Most groups have monthly business meetings at which the Treasurer is allocated time to present the monthly Treasurer's report. The report usually covers the previous month. For example, during the January business meeting the Treasurer will report on income and expenses for December. This typically consists of how much money was collected during the month, and how much was disbursed. The Treasurer might also discuss what upcoming expenses may need to be considered. The Treasurer typically also shares how much money is in the prudent reserve and any other savings categories. The Secretary usually records the report into the business meeting minutes.

If there is money available after the group's expenses and goals for its reserves are met, the Treasurer usually makes a motion regarding the balance that is available for contributions. See the "Suggested Contributions" section.

Sometimes the Treasurer supplies a one page copy of the monthly Treasurer's report (see example on next page) for future reference. Other copies can be provided for participating members at the business meeting. The Treasurer's report will also likely include a monthly comparison between the actual financial activity of the group and its group spending plan (again, see next page).

In addition to a monthly report, some Treasurers whose groups have a bank account bring copies of the bank statement to share with the group during the Treasurer's report. The income and expense form can also be used to report bank transactions and balances.

Sample Treasurer's Report and Spending Plan Comparison

GENERAL FUND		MONTHLY PLAN	APRIL ACTUAL	DIFFERENCE
INCOME				
	Weekly collections (Seventh Tradition)	300.00	322.26	22.26
	Unexpected income	0.00	0.00	0.00
		300.00	322.26	22.26
EXPENSES				
	Rent (Prudent reserve = $300 which is 3 months' rent)	100.00	100.00	0.00
	Newcomer packets (estimated at 12 per month)	20.00	0.00	20.00
	Copies and supplies (includes anniversary coins)	35.00	15.00	20.00
	Literature (for replacement of lost or stolen pamphlets)	10.00	0.00	10.00
	Group specific expenses			
	Group specific item #1	15.00	0.00	15.00
	Group specific item #2	15.00	0.00	15.00
	Accrued donations for John H. ($75) & WS Month ($105)	15.00	15.00	0.00
	Distributions (Income less expenses less reserves)			
	GSB donation (50% of previous month's excess)	45.00	75.00	(30.00)
	Intergroup donation (50% of previous month's excess)	45.00	75.00	(30.00)
		300.00	280.00	20.00
	Net Income / (loss) for period reported	0.00	42.26	

GSR FUND		MONTHLY PLAN	Dec-2014 ACTUAL	DIFFERENCE
INCOME				
	Weekly collections (GSR Fund)	175.00	160.00	(15.00)
	Fundraisers	0.00	0.00	0.00
	Unexpected income	0.00	0.00	0.00
		175.00	160.00	(15.00)
EXPENSES				
	Estimate only – Detailed spending plan will be developed when the registration packet is released.	175.00	0.00	175.00
		175.00	0.00	175.00
	Net Income / (loss) for period reported	0.00	160.00	

Feelings That May Come Up

Many Treasurers share that they feel nervous when presenting the Treasurer's Report at the monthly business meeting. Others have felt confused with the process of managing the treasury. Still others have determined that they need help to serve their group effectively or realize they cannot handle the money.

Members have found that speaking with sponsors, Pressure Relief Groups, and previous group Treasurers has been enormously helpful when these and any other issues come up while serving as Treasurer. Many find that being Treasurer offers an opportunity to practice humility, rigorous honesty, and asking for help, all of which contribute to our recovery.

We also find that electing an Assistant Treasurer and using a spending plan and standardized reporting (like the example on the previous page) can be very helpful.

Challenges and Resolutions

The following is a partial list of challenges that a group or Treasurer have experienced:

Challenge: No members who meet the group's requirements are willing to be the Treasurer.

Resolution: Have responsible members safeguard the funds while the group seeks a qualified member to be Treasurer.

Challenge: The only members who volunteer are newcomers or members who do not meet the group's requirements.

Resolution: Gently thank these volunteers for their willingness to serve and encourage them to try again after they have met the qualifications (that is, six months or a year of not incurring new unsecured debt and having had at least four Pressure Relief Meetings.)

Challenge: The Treasurer is not fulfilling their duties (that is, incomplete or vague records; records missing or destroyed; funds missing or stolen; funds inappropriately spent).

Resolution: When these problems arise, especially missing or stolen funds, groups are encouraged and supported in refraining from acting in a punitive way in observance of the Fifth warranty of D.A.'s Twelfth Concept, which states in part: "There should be no room for punishment in D.A. Love and service should be our motto."

Remember: There are always spiritual solutions which may include praying for the still-suffering former Treasurer. The financial challenge of rebuilding a group's Seventh Tradition funds is similar to that presented in starting a D.A. group, which is addressed in the D.A. Manual for Service.

Challenge: The Treasurer is overwhelmed and complains about doing the job.

Resolution: Form a PRG and have a PRM regarding the group's Treasurer position.

Challenge: The Treasurer does not want to have their name on the checking account.

Resolution: This may not be the right person for the position. If you choose to accept this condition of service, the new Treasurer can close the checking account and go on a cash basis. A new checking account can be opened in the future if the group decides to do that.

Challenge: The Treasurer disappears and is unreachable.

Resolution: If the person(s) eligible to sign on the account are not available, the bank has forms that the group secretary can complete with the help of the group, to obtain the funds. This often involves giving the bank typed minutes from the group's business meeting authorizing the action.

Challenge: The Treasurer does not want to give up the service.

Resolution: The Second Tradition is a good place to start for a solution: "For our group purpose there is but one ultimate authority--a loving God as He may express Himself in our group conscience. Our leaders are but trusted servants; they do not govern." In a group's business meeting, a group conscience could determine that the Treasurer's term of service has ended, elect a new Treasurer, and determine how to manage the transition. Understandably, this may be an emotional event for some members, but by following spiritual principles, the group conscience can determine the correct action.

Challenge: The group incurs unsecured debt.
Resolution: Form a PRG and have a PRM regarding the group's Treasurer position. The lack of solvency should be included in the Seventh Tradition announcement at every meeting until the debt is resolved.

ONCE MORE, REMEMBER: There are always spiritual solutions, and you are not alone in service.

Literature Resources for D.A. Treasurers

D.A. Pamphlets
— Recordkeeping
— Spending Plan
— Service
— Spirituality
— Business Meetings

D.A. Service Literature
— How to Keep Your Meeting Alive (Item GSB-1)
— Group Inventory: All Shapes and Sizes (Item GSB-3)
— G.S.O.: General Service Office of Debtors Anonymous (Item S-102)

A.A. Pamphlets
— Self-Support: Where Money and Spirituality Mix
— A.A. Group Treasurer

Frequently Asked Questions

What is the requirement to be the Treasurer of a D.A. group?

Each group establishes its own requirements. Many have found that six months or a year of not incurring new unsecured debt and having had at least four Pressure Relief Meetings is a good guideline for the group Treasurer position.

Does each D.A. group have to get a tax I.D. number to open a checking account?

In the United States, the Internal Revenue Service requires a group to get an Employer Identification Number (EIN) (also called a tax I.D. number) before it can open a checking account. This is a quick and easy process. See "Opening a Group Checking Account" for more information.

Can registered D.A. groups use the EIN and tax-exempt status of D.A. to open checking accounts so they do not have to incorporate as non-profit organizations?

Debtors Anonymous General Service Board, Inc. does not provide the corporation's 501(c)(3) tax-exempt status to individual D.A. groups. A group does not need to incorporate as a non-profit in order to open a checking account. See "Opening a Group Checking Account" for more information on how to obtain an employer identification number (EIN) and open a group checking account.

What are appropriate reimbursements for group expenses?

There may be times when a group member, other than the Treasurer, spends money on behalf of the group, for example to make copies of a flier for the group, or to reserve a meeting hall for a special event. It is important to give the trusted servant a clear guideline on how much has been planned for the expense and the maximum amount the group will reimburse.

It is also recommended that the group provide the funds in advance to the trusted servant who will procure goods or services so that the group does not become indebted to any member. If for some reason an exact amount cannot be determined beforehand, a contingency amount should be provided to the trusted servant so that no out of pocket expense is incurred.

Can a group have too much money?

After the group's needs are met, including GSR travel and the prudent reserve, it is suggested that groups contribute the balance remaining to the General Service Office, the local Intergroup, and the GSR Area Group. See the "Suggested Contributions" and sample Treasurer's Report sections for more information.

What can I do if my group is debting?

Groups which do not collect enough to pay their rent or other basic expenses may be debting or on the road to debting. Bringing the issue up at a business meeting is one place to start to address this issue at the group level. Some groups have found it helpful to study the Seventh Tradition of A.A. in the Twelve Steps and Twelve Traditions of Alcoholics Anonymous. Others have found that taking a group inventory and suggesting a higher contribution from members has been another way to break the cycle. Still other groups have moved the meeting to a venue that they could afford.

Can our group use online Bill Pay to send contributions to the GSO?

See section earlier in document titled "Online Bill Pay."

How can groups outside the USA make contributions to the GSO and purchase literature?

Currently, for Seventh Tradition contributions and literature orders from groups outside the United States, we require payment through: a) check in U.S. dollars drawn on a U.S. bank; or b) an international money order or bank draft. In many countries, the national post office/service sells international money orders, as do various commercial services.

Shipping costs for literature orders to Canada and other non-U.S. countries depend upon the total weight of the order and the country to which it will be shipped. Please send an email to the GSO, (office@debtorsanonymous.org), indicating the specific items and quantities you wish to order. The office will respond within three business days with details on shipping options and costs.

REMEMBER: The Treasurer position is one of great importance for every D.A. group. However, the Treasurer does not have to do this service alone. This manual, the D.A. Traditions, the Assistant Treasurer, and other group members can all offer help, insight, and support.

Revised by the 2011-2012 and 2012-2013 Resource Development Committees
Approved by the General Service Board, Oct. 2013

Appendix: Bill Pay Awareness Letter (approved and distributed 2013)

Your U.S. bank's Bill Pay service can be used to send contributions to the D.A. General Service Office

With the rise of electronic financial transactions, the General Service Board (GSB) and the World Service Conference (WSC) recognize that some D.A. members and groups want to make contributions to the General Service Office (GSO) electronically.

While D.A. members can make secure contributions via the D.A. website, the WSC Resource Development Committee would like to point out an alternative method of making electronic contributions that can be done automatically.

That is, most U.S. banks offer a Bill Pay service that will disburse checks at the accountholder's request. Using this service, a D.A. member could arrange to send a one-time contribution to the GSO or set up automatic recurring payments.

Just like individual D.A. members, D.A. groups with checking accounts could also use a Bill Pay service to make electronic contributions.

Instructions for setting up Bill Pay with your bank

The D.A. Treasurer's Manual provides these instructions for setting up Bill Pay capability:
The D.A. GSO is now currently equipped to arrange electronic funds transfers, but U.S. members and groups can also use the online Bill Pay service of their bank to send contributions to D.A. For members who do not have Internet access, most banks allow customers to fill out the paperwork in person at a branch office.

Arrange for online Bill Pay as follows:

The member or group should set up the payee as "DA-GSB" with the following address:

General Service Office
P.O. Box 920888
Needham, MA 02492-0009

If your bank's Bill Pay system has a memo field, include your email address there.

Once the setup has been completed, the member or group can then send funds anytime they want directly from their account.

If you're interested in using your bank's Bill Pay capability, contact your financial institution.

In gratitude and service,
The 2012-2013 WSC Resource Development Committee
Updated by the 2018-2019 Finance Committee

3. Business Meeting Chair

The Business Meeting Chair is the person who facilitates the group's regular monthly Business Meeting as well as any special business meetings that the group may decide to hold. Sometimes the group Chair, GSR, or Secretary serves as the Business Meeting Chair. Generally, the requirements to be a Business Meeting Chair are that the member has three to six months of not incurring unsecured debt, has had at least two Pressure Relief Meetings, and has a good working knowledge of the 12 Traditions of Debtors Anonymous. Many Business Meeting Chairs also find it is helpful to have some knowledge of parliamentary procedure, which is a set of rules for conduct at meetings that is helpful in allowing everyone to be heard and to enable the group to make decisions without confusion. Of course, each group can decide upon the eligibility requirements for its Business Meeting Chair by a group conscience. All decisions made by the Business Meeting or in relation to the Business Meeting are governed by Tradition Two.

It is important to note that some groups find it is beneficial to specifically designate someone to act as Business Meeting Chair, rather than having the Meeting Chair/Secretary serve dual roles. By designating a Business Meeting Chair, the group allows more members to be of service.

The Business Meeting Chair opens the Business Meeting with the Serenity Prayer and often reads Tool 10 from the 12 Tools of D.A, which states that "We attend business meeting that are held monthly. Many of us have long harbored feelings that 'business' was not a part of our lives, but for 'others' more qualified. Yet participation in running our own program teaches us how our organization operates, and also helps us to become responsible for our own recovery." If the service of a timekeeper is needed for the Business Meeting, the Business Meeting Chair asks for a volunteer to act as timekeeper during the Business Meeting; timing may be necessary if the group has decided to designate, for example, fifteen minutes for the reading of the Minutes of the previous Business Meeting and reports from the groups officers, fifteen minutes for old business, and fifteen minutes for new business.

Then, the Business Meeting Chair calls the Business Meeting to order.

Then, the Business Chair calls for a reading of the Minutes of the previous Business Meeting. The Business Meeting Secretary reads those Minutes (see description of the Business Meeting Secretary position below). The reading of the Minutes allows the group to review the Minutes for an accurate record of the proceedings of the previous business meeting and reminds members of outstanding old business that the group needs to consider at the current business meeting.

Next, the Business Meeting Chair will ask for all relevant reports by other trusted servants, such as the Treasurer and Literature Chairperson's report.

Next, the Business Chair introduces the first item of old business, unless there are elections that must be held or there is any other pressing item of business that the group conscience decides are necessary to address first, before the first item of old business, at that particular business meeting.

The first item of old business is subject to the usual parliamentary procedure—first, a motion is read and seconded about the item of business; after the motion has been made and seconded, discussion follows. Generally, the Business Meeting Chair is responsible for recognizing members who wish to speak and keeps the business meeting proceeding in an orderly manner. After the discussion of the motion is complete, the Business Meeting Chair asks that the motion be taken to a vote. The Business Meeting Chair asks for yea votes, no votes, and abstentions.

Other items of old business are then handled, usually in the order that they have been raised by members of the meeting and are listed in the Minutes of the previous Business Meeting. After old business has been addressed, the Business Meeting Chair will call for new business items. Some groups require that new business items be submitted to the Business Meeting Chair or the Business Meeting Secretary prior to the start of the Business Meetings to be added to the Business Meeting agenda. Other groups will allow members to raise new issues from the floor during the business meeting. Items of new business are also subject to the parliamentary procedures in the same manner as an item of old business, namely a motion is made, seconded, subject to discussion, and then, is voted upon.

For all items of old business and new business, the group observes Tradition 2 in that decisions reflect the group conscience or the consensus of the group. A group will decide if a majority vote or more than a majority vote constitutes the group conscience. Also, each group may decide that certain issues, such as changes to eligibility requirements for group officers, may require more than a majority vote, such as a two-thirds vote of members present.

At the appointed closing time for the Business Meeting, unless there has been a group conscience to extend the time for the Business Meeting, or when all pending business is completed, the Business Meeting Chair asks for a motion to close the Business Meeting, which must be seconded and approved by the group. The Business Meeting Chair then closes the Business Meeting with a final prayer.

4. Business Meeting Secretary

Some groups also select a Business Meeting Secretary. This officer assists the Business Meeting Chair and keeps Minutes of the business meetings. In some larger meetings, the Business Meeting Secretary prepares an agenda for upcoming business meetings, if the protocol for that meeting is that new motions or items of business are submitted by members prior to the Business Meeting. The Secretary may also be responsible for posting the Minutes in a notebook where all previous Business Meeting Minutes are kept for reference.

Unlike many other service positions, this important position is open to all members, as there are generally no requirements to serve as Business Meeting Secretary. Therefore, often newcomers are encouraged to take on this service.

At some meetings, the Business Meeting Secretary is also responsible for maintaining a list of the names and contact information of the officers of the meeting.

5. Intergroup Service Representative
The Intergroup Service Representative position is discussed in greater detail in Chapter 3.

6. General Service Representative

The General Service Representative position is discussed in greater detail in Chapter 5.

7. Public Relations/Outreach Coordinator

The position of Public Information Representative is discussed in greater detail in Chapter 4.

E. How to Keep Your Meeting Alive

When a new Debtors Anonymous meeting is started in a city or town that formerly had none, a sense of hope and enthusiasm motivates the founding members for some months. These individuals feel that the answer to their money problems is at hand. They rightfully believe that meetings can relieve them of the overwhelming debt in which they find themselves. Although they are not exactly sure how this miracle will happen, these sincere newcomers make a commitment to their recovery and to starting a meeting.

Sometimes the group is fortunate enough to have an experienced D.A. member move to their community from an area with a large number of Debtors Anonymous meetings. This member will often bring a solid knowledge of the recovery process to the meeting and the meeting thrives as time passes. Not all groups are this fortunate. Some groups do their best to build their meeting, but over time the group stays small and eventually closes. The founders of the meeting complain, "I started a meeting but no one came."

This comment raises two questions. Were the efforts to reach a core group of still-suffering debtors thorough and persistent? If the answer is unequivocally "Yes," then we must ask "Why are we not retaining members?"

In answering these two questions, we can focus on the dynamics that prevent the closing of groups. They have worked for other D.A. meetings, and will work for your group. Both the externals of the meeting and the internal spiritual condition of the founding members are important to consider.

External factors

One factor that makes a meeting successful is as simple as making sure the meeting is easy to find. Can people get to your meeting easily, and when they find you, is parking available? Is the meeting at a time and place that is convenient for members? Is there a sign placed on the correct entrance and other signs directing people to the correct room? Has the meeting been announced in the community pages of the newspaper or on cable TV giving the time, place, and a one-line description of D.A.? Is the meeting location accessible for a wide variety of mobility needs? Is the room the right size for the group? When a group of six to eight people meet in a large auditorium, it emphasizes the smallness of the group. For this reason alone, people may not return.

Questions to Consider

- Why do meetings disband?

- What specific precautions against meeting death can a meeting take?

- Does my behavior drive newcomers away?

- Do I introduce myself to newcomers and let them know they can recover?

When people first arrive at the meeting, does someone greet them and introduce them to other members? Is there literature for them to take away? The General Service Office has available a leaflet called "Notes to Newcomers," which can be duplicated by groups and given away for free. Do members of the group give newcomers personal attention and encouragement?

Some ways to do this are: a) appoint greeters for each meeting who can talk to newcomers during the break or after the meeting; b) offer transportation help, if needed; c) encourage the newcomer to join you for coffee after the meeting; d) befriend the newcomer even if they don't ask you to be their sponsor; e) help newcomers get involved in service as soon as possible; let them know how they can help the meeting thrive.

If the meeting is at night, would refreshments meet the needs of those attending? One Friday night meeting that attracts members from a fifty-mile radius serves coffee and food at the meeting. Debtors will return to a meeting that recognizes their need for hospitality and welcome. Do members give out their phone numbers and take the phone numbers of newcomers, giving them a friendly call during the week? This service increases the likelihood that the newcomer will return. Some groups develop a written and duplicated phone list giving first name and last initial, phone number, and best time to call. These are available for newcomers. One of the most powerful indicators of whether a group will survive is if the members call each other between meetings.

It is very tempting to neglect the collection of a Seventh Tradition when the group is small and meeting in a private home. This will doom the group to certain failure as it perpetuates individual debting at a group level. A second vital practice for group survival is the development of a group spending plan. Even if the group collects less than two dollars a week, a spending plan can be developed that meets the group's expenses of rent, contributions to the General Service Office or local Intergroup. By creating a spending plan for the group, we are demonstrating recovery from the vagueness of debting.

When potential members do not return, is it because they do not see or hear in us examples of what recovery from compulsive debting looks like? Do they hear a litany of problems and a refrain of negative remarks about creditors or life in general? Do we sound like victims or victors? Do we talk about the problem or do we remember to present the solution in our sharing? Yes, we all have problems, but if we will remember to describe how the Tools and the Steps of the program have improved our lives, newcomers will see in us an exciting picture of recovery from debting.

Internal factors

What if many efforts to reach debtors in the community have been made, yet individuals come a few times and then fall away?

A second group of factors to consider is concerned with the internal condition of the core members. Some D.A. members are overly responsible and try to help every person who walks in the door. If you recognize this in yourself and are too busy to sponsor a newcomer who approaches you, introduce them to other members of the group who may help. If a newcomer does not follow through, do not take it personally.

Are we realistic about the times we tell a member to call? If we are never home at night, does it make sense to imply that we will be available for them? If a person stops calling, find out why by calling them. Perhaps they feel they have failed the group or program and you can reassure them.

Sometimes, the founding member of a group gives in to the temptation to dominate the group, driving away those who are sensitive or resistant to control. It is understandable that an individual member who has donated a great deal of time, energy, and passion in starting and maintaining a meeting would feel that group decisions should go their way. This can be identified by working Steps Four through Nine and must be resisted at all costs.

Conclusion

Recovery from debting does not take place in a vacuum. Meetings are the vehicle for debtors to find the help they need to stop debting, share their successes and problems, laugh at their compulsion, and give to others what they have received from the program and their Higher Power. Every meeting can be a strong meeting.

F. Sponsor-A-Group

Sponsor-A-Group is modeled after individual sponsorship to help connect strong and well-resourced groups with groups that are either just getting started or are in need of additional guidance and support. This group-to-group sponsorship exists between two D.A. meetings: A D.A. Sponsor Group and a D.A. Sponsee Group.

- D.A. Sponsor Group is an established D.A. meeting with recovery and solvency that shares experience, strength, and hope including practical D.A. resources with a D.A. Sponsee Group

- D.A. Sponsee Group partners with an experienced D.A. Sponsor Group to receive guidance to start a new meeting or to strengthen an existing meeting.

- Each Sponsor-A-Group match identifies together what are the most important needs of the Sponsee Group and what support can be offered by the Sponsor Group. Together, the Sponsor and Sponsee Group determine an 'action plan' for moving forward.

For more information, visit www.debtorsanonymous.org/sponsor-a-group

G. The Seventh Tradition: How to Contribute to Our Fellowship

What is D.A.'s Seventh Tradition?

Just like your own group, the GSO is self-supporting through the contributions of D.A. groups and members everywhere. The Seventh Tradition is a Spiritual activity that connects us to every member of the Fellowship around the World. The GSO cannot serve you or any suffering compulsive debtor without your personal and your group's experience, strength, hope, and financial support. The GSO must serve a rapidly growing number of members like you and groups like yours, and it cannot do so without adequate funds and prudent reserves. Each D.A. member and each group is asked to provide regular support at every level so each D.A. member, each group and the GSO can do the most important task that any of us has: to carry the message to the still-suffering compulsive debtor.

How do my contributions help D.A.?

Contributions support the General Service Office (GSO), help publish literature and other materials. In addition, the World Service and General Service Board Committees provide services to the

Fellowship to carry the message. In addition, contributions make sure that the General Service Office is staffed, supplied, and services from shipping literature to answering phone calls is provided.

How can I make a personal contribution?

Each individual D.A. member who is able is asked to contribute at each meeting so the local group has enough funds to pay rent, buy literature, sponsor special events, build a prudent reserve, and contribute to any Area Group, any Intergroup, and the GSB. Even if you are unable to give, please keep coming back. The still-suffering debtor is the most important person in D.A. and all the efforts of both the GSO and the GSB serve you and help you and all compulsive debtors like you recover. Members who have experienced prosperity through recovery in D.A. are asked to put $5 in the basket at each meeting. At the WSC in 2018, the Conference voted to increase the maximum individual yearly contribution to the Fellowship to $12,000 USD. Members may also make additional contributions to the John H. Scholarship Fund. Because John H. Scholarship funds are used to support delegates (GSRs and ISRs) who attend the annual WSC, these donations are not counted toward the annual $12,000 USD limit.

Individuals may want to give directly to the GSB on a regular basis or to celebrate special occasions such as:

- Prosperity contributions. If you receive a new job or a raise, pay off a debt, resolve a legal issue successfully, or are blessed in any other way through your recovery in D.A., you may want to express your gratitude with a contribution.

- Anniversary Gifts. Many D.A. members give special gifts to the GSB to commemorate the anniversary of their first D.A. meeting or their first day of not incurring unsecured debt.

- Regular contributions. Many D.A. members put monthly or quarterly contributions to the GSB, above and beyond their group donations, in their personal spending plans.

How can I make an online contribution?

An alternative to mailing contributions to the GSB is D.A.'s online contribution feature which accepts United States bank-issued Debit Cards and some internationally issued cards. You can access this feature at: www.debtorsanonymous.org/donate. Fill in the requested information then press the "Submit Payment" button. You will receive an acknowledgement for your contribution to the email address you provided which will serve as a receipt.

In addition, Debtors Anonymous offers an electronic method of processing contributions from outside the United States. Through D.A.'s link with Wise (wise.com) contributions can be transferred from overseas, converted to US Dollars and deposited into Bank of America's Debtors Anonymous account. Currently, D.A. is able to accept contributions in British Pounds, Euros, Australian Dollars and New Zealand Dollars. Using Wise, bank charges are eliminated and the only cost to contributors is the currency exchange fee. Other countries who can pay in the approved currencies into any of those accounts can also use Wise from their banks with their currency.

Contact the Office to obtain the current transferring instructions for Wise as they can change periodically.

Where does D.A.'s income come from? Where does D.A.'s money go?

The graphs below and on the following page are for the 12-month period of July 1, 2015 through June 30, 2016. For more recent reports, refer to current issues of *the DA Focus*.

Debtors Anonymous General Service Board, Inc.
July 2015 – June 2016

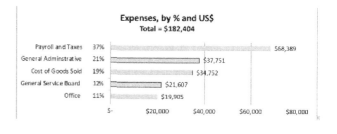

* Interest, World Service Month contributions, and Audio-Visual sales

Interest, World Service Month contributions, and Audio-Visual sales

Debtors Anonymous General Service Board, Inc.
July 2015 – June 2016

Revenue, by Source

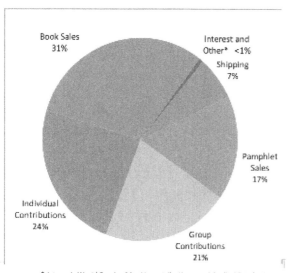

* Interest, World Service Month contributions, and Audio-Visual sales

Expenses, by Category

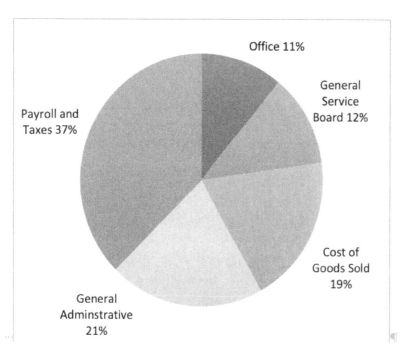

How can my meeting contribute?

We suggest your group establish a group spending plan and a local treasury with adequate prudent reserves, usually three months of normal expenses. Meet your local expenses first to keep the meeting healthy. Divide any surplus—each month—by the following recommended formula: if your area has an Intergroup, contribute 50% of any surplus to Intergroup, and 50% to the GSB. If your area has an Intergroup and an Area Group of GSRs, then contribute 45% to Intergroup, 45% to the GSB and 10% to the Area Group. If your area does NOT have either an Intergroup or an Area Group, contribute 100% of the surplus to the GSB. Each treasurer should send a contribution by check or money order after the group's monthly business meeting.

How can my Intergroup contribute?

Intergroups are asked to contribute 100% of their surplus to the GSB.

What can my Area Group do?

Area Groups are asked to contribute 100% of their surplus to the GSB.

Collecting contributions for special events [1]

Many groups and Intergroups pass a special basket to support the GSB during special events, such as Fellowship Days, World Service Month, group anniversaries, etc.

Where do I send my contribution?

Please make your check or money order payable to "D.A.-GSB" and mail to D.A. GSO, PO Box 920888, Needham, MA 02492-0009. Checks or money orders should be in US Funds.

H. Group Inventory: All Shapes and Sizes

All shapes and sizes of D.A. groups and meetings can benefit from a written inventory. Some groups occasionally or regularly take a "group inventory" using an entire meeting for an honest and fearless discussion of the group's weaknesses and strengths. It is wise to plan and announce this some months in advance and to ask former members to come back for the inventory to share why they stopped coming. Usually a facilitator is obtained from another meeting. He or she will chair the group inventory, making sure that a positive tone is maintained at all times throughout the process and that a fair discussion is held.

The format of the meeting can vary according to the size and wishes of the meeting. One large city meeting has developed a format, used annually, that provides three minutes for each member of the group wishing to speak. Members can share the things they like about the meeting and improvements they would like to see. This is a balanced inventory, similar to the Fourth Step inventory we take as individuals. It helps to see that the group has assets. Building upon our good features is a strong way to develop our meeting.

The secretary of the meeting records in writing all the suggestions for improvement. During the next month, the secretary consolidates and compiles the suggestions and organizes them into a list. The list is photocopied and then presented at a special, pre-announced business meeting. Members eliminate the unrealistic suggestions and select the most feasible and urgent. These are then rank-ordered and the group decides upon a few goals to work on. Volunteers can develop an action plan and see that the changes are made. The inventory has paid off. It has provided a vehicle for expressing Tradition Two:

> *For our group purpose there is but one ultimate authority—a loving God as He may express Himself in our group conscience.*

Another type of group inventory is based upon a list of questions that address the functioning of

---

1   See also "A Guide to Special Events" in section G of this chapter.

the group. This might be more appropriate for a small group. This method forestalls the fear or embarrassment most members feel at bringing up sensitive topics. An experienced chairperson leads the group through each question, allowing anyone to speak on the topic. For weeks in advance, members and visitors are given a list of inventory questions similar to the list given on the next page. The group secretary records the comments, organizes them by topic, types them up and brings them to a business meeting for discussion and possible development of an action plan through group consensus. In this way, groups become stronger and all members benefit from the power of truth.

At one group inventory meeting conducted with a list of questions, a one-time visitor from another part of the country was able to participate in the inventory by contributing their impressions of the meeting from a valuable perspective, that of the first-time attendee. When still-suffering debtors attend their first meeting, they will form a decision about whether to return based upon our behavior.

Intergroups and the General Service Board of Trustees also conduct group inventories, both on their individual attitudes and behavior and on the way the group functions in fulfilling their service duties. At every level of service, inventories are a good idea!

You can develop your own questions for a group inventory or use these:

Meetings

1. Do we have a group spending plan?
2. Is the principle of anonymity maintained, avoiding gossip?
3. How can our sponsorship be improved?
4. Do all members take responsibility for the physical housekeeping for the group?
5. Do we use only conference-approved literature at our meetings, or have we allowed outside literature to creep in?
6. Do we focus on the positive benefits of the D.A. Program, making sure to be an example of what the program can do to help us?
7. Do we have a clearly defined way of sharing power, or does all power reside in the hands of a favored few?
8. Do we have an up-to-date GSO contact who keeps the group informed, or do mailings from the General Service Board get ignored?
9. Do we donate to the Intergroup, Area Group, and General Service Office?

Group Business Meetings

1. Do we use the tools of the program for the group welfare as well as our own?
2. Does each and every member have an opportunity to participate in group activities?
3. Are service people chosen with care and consideration, placing principles before personalities, for the welfare of the group as a whole?
4. Do we enlist newcomers in service positions just to make sure they keep coming to the meeting?
5. Are we unafraid to discuss money matters at the group business meetings?
6. Do we keep the General Service Office informed of any changes in our meeting time and place?
7. Do we let the General Service Office know when our group contact is no longer available?
8. Do we even have a group contact person? Do we know who he or she is?
9. Do we have a General Service Representative (GSR) and have we established a GSR travel fund in the group spending plan?
10. Is business conducted in an orderly manner at our business meetings?

Intergroup Business Meetings

1. Are we reaching the debtors in our community?
2. Do we use the Business Owners Debtors Anonymous tools for the functioning of our group?
3. Is there more that the Intergroup can do to carry the message to the debtor who still suffers?
4. Do we sell only conference-approved literature at our annual day-long conferences?
5. Do we have excessive turnover of Intergroup Service Representatives?
6. Have we attempted to find out why members are not interested in doing service?

I. A Guide to Special Events

Debtors Anonymous groups sometimes have a special event outside of the normal meeting time. The event might or might not have the purpose of raising funds. In either case, there are a variety of goals for special events, but it is recommended that all events:

- Be open to all D.A. members including newcomers

- Be closed to the general public

- Uphold the Twelve Traditions

- Enhance fellowship

- Offer something of value to the participants

- Share service responsibilities

- Not require that donations be mandatory, though they may be suggested

Just as the Twelve Steps, Twelve Traditions, and Twelve Tools provide the path for our personal recovery, they also provide the framework for a successful event.

Event Suggestions

In keeping with the Fourth Tradition, it is suggested that an event not be represented as a "D.A. event" since that would imply it was approved by the whote Fellowship. An acceptable alternative example would be a "12-Step Workshop given by the Wednesday Night Serenity group of Debtors Anonymous."

Debtors Anonymous members are creative and there is no limit to the breadth of topics and formats for special events. A few suggested topics that can be relied upon for events are:

- Working the Twelve Steps

- Living the Traditions

- Sponsoring and Being Sponsored

- Keeping the Numbers

- Pressure Relief Meeting Workshop

- Visions Workshop

- Fellowship with a silent auction

- BDA Business Planning Workshop

- Speaker Panel with ask-it basket and audience members sharing:
  - Long-timer's sharing – How I did it
  - 12-Step sharing of experience, strength, and hope
  - How the Twelve Promises have come true
  - Sharing recovery miracles
  - Life after debt

The Steps and Tools

Although all the D.A. Tools are useful for creating a successful event, a few are highlighted here to help members plan.

Service

Generally, a core group of dedicated members will organize the event and bring it to fruition. They are performing 12-Step service and are the trusted servants for the event. This steering committee will often try to include volunteers with all levels of D.A. experience so the service load will be shared and members get the benefits of performing service.

Action Plan

The more detailed and specific the action plan for the event, the less likely it will be that unforeseen logistics or circumstances could create "chaos and drama." The event plan also clarifies what actions each member doing service will perform and when they will do their part. However, even the most detailed of planning allows opportunity for Higher Power to create what no one may have predicted in that planning.

Spending Plan and Awareness

Whether or not the event has the goal of raising funds, it will have expenses. Just as we do with our personal or business finances, we create a spending plan for the event. The spending plan and the tool of awareness ensure that any member authorized to spend funds for the event will have a clear idea of how much to spend for their task. This clarity avoids situations where a well-meaning but misinformed member may spend more than the group can afford on materials for the event, such as flyers or decorations. The spending plan allows for abundance for the event within the sobriety of clarity around the numbers.

The Telephone and the Internet

In addition to announcing the event at D.A. meetings, the telephone and the internet are effective ways of spreading the word and facilitating the event planning. In this context, anonymity concerns should be borne in mind.

The Traditions and Events

All the Traditions are important guides for planning and carrying out events. A few are highlighted here for consideration.

Tradition Five

Each group has but one primary purpose—to carry its message to the debtor who still suffers.

By maintaining focus on the Fifth Tradition, the planning group will ensure that the event will truly provide 12-step service.

Tradition Six

A D.A. group ought never endorse, finance, or lend the D.A. name to any related facility or outside enterprise, lest problems of money, property, and prestige divert us from our primary purpose.

The more mindful the event committee is of this Tradition when deciding on the format and venue for the event, the more successful the event will be. This Tradition is also critical for spreading the word for the event to other D.A. members while being careful not to imply an association or authorization for the event by Debtors Anonymous as a whole. This Tradition also is a good reminder to avoid topics from outside sources and to avoid using non-conference approved literature at events.

Tradition Seven

Every D.A. group ought to be fully self-supporting, declining outside contributions.

Events are sometimes held with the intent of raising funds to send the group's GSR to the annual Debtors Anonymous World Service Conference. When selling tickets to an event such as this, it is important that it only be promoted to members of D.A., ensuring that an outside contribution is not inadvertently accepted from a person that is not a member of the fellowship.

Tradition Eight

Debtors Anonymous should remain forever non-professional, but our service centers may employ special workers.

This Tradition reminds the committee to avoid any compensation to D.A. members acting as members of PRG's or any other service that might be seen as Twelfth Step work. A suggested donation to the event would be more appropriate than charging members for services.

Tradition Nine

D.A., as such, ought never be organized; but we may create service boards or committees directly responsible to those they serve.

This Tradition is a good reminder to the trusted servants on the event planning committee and the people providing service during the event that they are responsible to the members attending the event.

How-To Suggestions

In addition to the previous general guidelines, the following specific ideas are offered to groups to use as they wish.

12-Step Workshop

Create a fellowship event where D.A. members experienced in working the 12 Steps share their experience, strength, and hope. Depending on the size of the group and the availability of qualified speakers, there could be one speaker per step or a speaker could cover a number of steps. Some larger groups or Intergroups may consider holding weekend-long workshops or retreats to work the Steps.

12 Promises Workshop

Similar to the 12-Step Workshop, a group could put on an event where the speakers share about how the 12 Promises of Debtors Anonymous have manifested in their lives. The workshop could include an ask-it basket for newcomers to ask any questions they may have. It is also recommended that time be allowed for sharing by members of the audience.

Pressure Relief Meeting Marathon

A group may organize a fellowship day focused on participating in Pressure Relief Groups (PRGs). The event may start with a speakers' panel sharing their experience, strength, and hope from giving and receiving PRGs. Then newcomers or others needing to receive a PRG are grouped with two other members qualified to give a PRG. After the first round of PRGs, there may be a break or a shared lunch. In the next session, the remaining members wanting to receive a PRG are grouped with those available to give. In some cases, those who received a PRG for the first time in the first session are able to give a PRG along with an experienced member in the second session. When planning an event of this type, it is recommended to get the word out so there are enough experienced members available to give to the newcomers. Also, it should be made clear to all in attendance that no fee should be charged for a Pressure Relief Meeting.

Additional Suggestions

Dance Party

Some D.A. groups and local areas have had successful dance parties. Other groups had fun dance parties but had disappointing attendance and were unable to recover all the costs. It is suggested that a group considering a dance party seek out the experience of other D.A. groups that have put on successful dance parties.

11th Step Meditation

Create an event with the focus on the 11th Step. Format could be a speaker, or possibly a walking meditation or having meditative music.

Retreat Day or Weekend

Many of the topics could be covered in the form of an all-day retreat or weekend. It is suggested that groups seek out the experience of other D.A. groups that have put on successful retreats.

Talent Show

D.A. is blessed with an abundance of talented members. A talent show is a fun way for D.A. members to perform and share their talents.

Vision Boards (a.k.a. Collages or Treasure Maps)

Have an event where members bring magazines and supplies to create their own Vision Board in the presence and support of other members. Everyone is encouraged to share their results with the group.

Garage Sales – Proceed with Caution!

If a group were to choose to hold a garage sale to the public and have signs saying it was a fundraiser for Debtors Anonymous, most D.A. members would agree that this would be a clear violation of the Traditions.

However, if a member, or members, of a group decided to hold a garage sale (anonymously) on their own, then donate the proceeds to the group's GSR Fund, many people would agree that this would not violate the Traditions. An important distinction to remember is that this garage sale is an "outside issue" and should not be announced at group level, nor should flyers promoting it be distributed at D.A. meetings.

In addition to being careful regarding the Traditions, D.A. members ought to also be aware that many D.A. members have difficulty with compulsive spending, and therefore a garage sale might not be the best format for a D.A. special event.

Applying These Principles

The Fourth Tradition states that each group is autonomous except in matters affecting other groups or D.A. as a whole, and the Second Tradition reminds us that the ultimate authority is our Higher Power expressed through our group conscience. With these and all the Traditions in mind, how each group decides to implement the Traditions in the planning and carrying out an event may be different. The examples provided are intended for reflective contemplation, not as a definitive interpretation of the Traditions and events.

Suggested Resources:

- "Spending Plan" pamphlet, available through GSO as item P-106

- The Twelve Traditions of Debtors Anonymous

CHAPTER 3 – INTERGROUP SERVICE

A. What is the Purpose of an Intergroup? [1]

Together we can accomplish what none of us could accomplish separately. This is the simple principle underlying the need for Intergroups. The primary purpose of any group is to carry the message of recovery to the still-suffering debtor. In many instances, a group operating by itself cannot do this effectively. Thus, a group of 10 or 12 members would find it both expensive and difficult to undertake creation of a "hot line," or even a telephone line and answering machine, for inquiries by potential members. One group might not be able to take advantage of quantity discounts in buying literature from the GSO. These activities, so important in carrying the message, can be facilitated through creation of an Intergroup.

Beyond this basic and fundamental purpose, an Intergroup can serve as a clearinghouse for information. Groups can send representatives to general meetings of an Intergroup and share their experience, strength, and hope in carrying the message. New ideas and approaches can be exchanged. Groups can learn what is happening elsewhere in their area and share their knowledge and experience with new or struggling groups.

Intergroups can also provide opportunities for cooperation in fellowship projects beyond the capacity of any one group. Thus, many Intergroups sponsor days of sharing which enable debtors to come together and exchange their recovery, unity, and service stories. A day-long program with workshops and individual speakers and the opportunity for sharing over coffee or lunch can provide an inexpensive and helpful respite for the newcomer still struggling with their debting.

Public information is another function that an Intergroup can perform that might be difficult for an individual group. Contacting the local media and making them aware of the existence and purpose of D.A. is sometimes hard for a small group. The same is true for contacting professionals, such as therapists and clergy, to inform them about the help available in D.A. Intergroups can also schedule training sessions for group media or PI contacts, to share experiences in carrying the message to these people. Some Intergroups have purchased literature, particularly *A Currency of Hope* and *The Twelve Steps, Twelve Traditions and Twelve Concepts of Debtors Anonymous* to distribute to public libraries. In some regions, members are trying to carry the message to those in prison (and other institutions) who, all too frequently, have struggled with earning and spending problems while outside the walls.

Intergroups also participate in the general service structure of D.A. Each Intergroup is entitled to select one Intergroup Service Representative (ISR) to attend the annual World Service Conference (WSC). The ISR serves as the link between the Intergroup, the WSC, and the General Service Board and GSO. The ISR carries the opinion of the Intergroup on world service matters to the Conference and shares the results of the Conference deliberations with the Intergroup. Each Intergroup should try to create a spending plan to send its ISR to the WSC on a regular basis.

Some large Intergroups have opened offices, at which they sell D.A. literature at discounted prices, possible because of quantity discounts available from the GSO. Others have published local meeting lists that can provide more detailed and current information than is available from the D.A. website.

Recently, Intergroups have partnered with the General Service Board in holding Regional Forums. In 2009, the first of these Forums was held in Boston. In 2010, forums were held in Minneapolis, Los Angeles, and Phoenix. In 2011, two Forums were hosted in New York and San Francisco. 2012 saw Forums in Charlotte, Chicago and Houston. They provide an opportunity for debtors throughout a wide area to come together with members of the General Service Board to share about the activities of the Board and GSO. Extensive opportunities are presented for Q&A sessions about D.A.'s finances, literature, and office operations and there are workshops on

---

1   The Intergroup Service Handbook, available on the D.A. website under "Resources for Meetings and Groups," shares best practices for Intergroups and how meetings can join together to start an Intergroup.

Intergroup service, the Traditions and D.A. history. These Regional Forums will be held in other locations in future years; it is hoped that a regular rotation throughout the United States at a dozen or more locations over a four-year period will be possible. In the future, as finances permit, international forums may also be scheduled.

B. How to Start an Intergroup

1. Contact Other Established Intergroups for Experience, Strength, and Hope

The starting point for creation of an Intergroup is, as always in D.A., with the individual local groups and their members. It is essential that several groups in an area agree upon the need and purpose of an Intergroup association. Without such group level support, an Intergroup can neither grow nor flourish. To develop such support, it is important to collect information from other, established Intergroups. You can find contact information for all Intergroups in existence at the D.A. website, www.debtorsanonymous.org. This information should include experience in establishing the Intergroup, costs of operation, spending plans, successful and unsuccessful programs, and suggestions as to rent, insurance, and location. The World Service Conference Intergroup Caucus would also be an excellent resource.

The names and current website addresses of active Intergroups can be found on the D.A. website. GSO provides these links to facilitate information about local D.A. activities. Our website links do not constitute or indicate review, endorsement, or approval by the D.A. GSB.

2. Create a Framework

Once the groups in an area have voted to create an Intergroup, the next step is to have each group elect an Intergroup Representative to participate in creating the framework within which the Intergroup will operate. Many have found that incorporating the Intergroup is a good idea, although this is not always necessary (most U.S. states recognize unincorporated associations as valid legal entities). As a general rule, if the Intergroup is going to hire employees or purchase equipment, experience has shown that incorporation may be the better route. It is always best to consult with an attorney to explore different possibilities.

The basic documents should outline the purposes of the Intergroup in general terms, the area served, the powers of the corporation, and any limits on those powers. Depending on local rules, it may also include the names of initial directors, place of incorporation, and any local requirements for service of process. If incorporation is the route chosen, the usual experience is to incorporate as a nonprofit corporation and to comply with requirements of the U.S. Internal Revenue Code applicable to nonprofits. In addition, the directors should adopt bylaws that outline in greater detail the structure of the organization, the duties and qualifications of its officers and Board, its relation to the groups, meeting requirements, committee structure, and method of amendment.

It is also important to remember that, in the United States, and in most states, there are filing requirements that any nonprofit body must comply with. Thus, tax returns and/or informational filings may be required. This usually does not present a problem with anonymity under the Eleventh Tradition, since these filings are not at the level of press, radio, television, or other major media. It is always desirable to consult with an experienced attorney to find out what might be necessary. The intricacies of not-for-profit corporate law can be difficult. The Intergroup also might wish to qualify as a 501(c)(3) group under the United States Internal Revenue Code so that it may take advantage of certain privileges available to those groups. Again, the help of an attorney is recommended. For Intergroups outside the U.S.A., please consult your local taxation authority.

In initial meetings, Intergroup Representatives should also be asked to provide direction on the areas in which the Intergroup can focus its efforts. An informational or "hot line" is one option. Others, including public information and outreach, may follow.

Intergroup Representatives should also be consulted when the officers adopt a spending plan for the Intergroup. This should be one of the first actions taken after the organization is formed. Every effort should be made to create a balanced and accurate spending plan. It is always better to err on the side of caution, and to avoid incurring expenses that are unclear or uncertain. Especially in the beginning, when experience does not yet exist, a manageable plan of action should be followed.

3. Register with D.A.

You may use the same online form used to re-register a group at https://debtorsanonymous.org/register

4. Find a Location

Most Intergroups do not have a physical office or space that they rent. Instead, they operate out of the home of one of their officers. In such a case, it is usually best that the Intergroup rent a Post Office box to receive mail. If possible, the Intergroup should also arrange for a separate telephone line in its own name. If these steps are followed, many difficulties with anonymity can be avoided. It is also easier to arrange for a change in access when officers rotate out of their positions and new officers take over. Even if the Intergroup operates out of the home of an officer, it is probably better that meetings of Intergroup Representatives be held elsewhere. A local church, school, or public library may provide an acceptable venue at a reasonable rate. This prevents the Intergroup from becoming associated with one person and assures that principles will come before personalities. Much of what has been said about group meeting places will also apply here.

If a physical office is within the spending plan of the Intergroup, it should be as attractive and well-lighted as possible. In planning for an office, it is important to remember that insurance may be necessary in addition to rent. For the protection of all in the case of an accident, efforts should be made to obtain such insurance. The size of any office space will depend upon a weighing of finances and needs. It is usually not necessary to plan on holding large meetings at the office space.

5. Elect Officers and Form Committees

The final step in forming an Intergroup is the election of officers and the formation of committees. Most Intergroups hold an annual or semi-annual meeting at which the Intergroup Representatives select a Chair, Vice Chair, Secretary, and Treasurer. The duties of Intergroup officers are similar to those of group officers, discussed above. The Treasurer may want to open a checking account, discussed above. Note that the D.A. General Service Office has a policy not to share the EIN number of the non-profit. Additionally, every Intergroup should have a Public Information Representative (PIR), whose job is to Chair the Public Information Committee. The functions of the Public Information Representative are discussed in greater detail in Chapter 5.

Some Intergroups may grow so large and undertake so much in the way of Twelfth Step work that they find it necessary to hire a full- or part-time employee to direct these activities. Finally, every Intergroup should select an Intergroup Service Representative (ISR), whose function is similar to that of a GSR at the group level. ISRs serve as the link between the Intergroup and the World Service Conference, representing the views of the Intergroup at the Conference and relaying back to the Intergroup the ongoing activities of the GSB, GSO, and the Conference. Each Intergroup should try to send its ISR to the World Service Conference as often as possible.

Some Intergroups select a Service Board, or Steering Committee, whose function is to supervise and coordinate the activities of the Intergroup on an ongoing basis. These Committees may meet monthly (or more frequently in an emergency), as opposed to the quarterly or semi-annual meetings of Intergroup Representatives. Steering committees are usually composed of the elected officers and committee chairs/coordinators. They report to the Intergroup Representatives at their quarterly or semi-annual meetings.

Committees are the groups through which most of an Intergroup's activities will be performed. The Public Information Committee, together with the PIR, plans and carries out local D.A. efforts to reach out to the community and inform people of D.A.'s existence and its program of recovery. This may be accomplished on many levels, including work with the media, professionals, corrections officials, and therapists. For more information, see the discussion of public information efforts in Chapter 4.

Other committees may include an event planning committee, a "hot line" committee, a web/InfoTech committee, a meeting list committee, a literature committee, and a resources/finance committee. Usually, each committee is headed by a coordinator or chair, who may serve on the Intergroup's Steering Committee. Additional committees may be established to reflect local needs.

The Event Planning Committee is responsible for scheduling, planning, and hosting those special events that the Intergroup decides to hold. These may include fellowship days, special workshops, pressure relief meeting workshops, Regional Forums (with the GSB), spiritual breakfasts, or other events open to the D.A. membership and designed to promote D.A. unity through the Traditions, while sharing experience, strength, and hope in recovery. The "hot line" committee is ordinarily responsible for monitoring the Intergroup answering machine and, in those areas where there is a large pool of volunteers available, answering the telephone. The web/InfoTech committee will frequently be responsible for formulating policies governing the website, ensuring that the postings are in conformity with the Traditions, and coordinating all information posted on the Internet. It may also include a webmaster and data base administrator.

The resources/finance committee is responsible for monitoring and preparing the Intergroup's spending plan and coordinating resource development. The meeting list committee is generally responsible for maintaining and updating the local meeting list, so that newcomers can be confident of finding a meeting. It may also be of great assistance to the General Service Office by providing notification when a meeting moves or is discontinued. The literature committee may order literature from GSO in bulk at a discount and resell the literature to local groups, saving time and postage for those groups.

Once the Intergroup has been organized, has found a place to work, has registered with GSO, and has selected its officers and committees, it is ready to begin its work of carrying the message of recovery to the still-suffering debtor.

CHAPTER 4 – PUBLIC INFORMATION OUTREACH

A. Public Information Manual

The World Service Conference (WSC) has approved the text of a Public Information Manual that is an invaluable tool for anyone interested in public information work. Not only does it contain the suggestions and guidelines reproduced below, but it also provides sample letters to the media, professionals and others that have been carefully edited to comply with the requirements of the Twelve Traditions. This document is based on the initial pages of the Public Information Manual.[1]

Introduction

The WSC Public Information (PI) Committee of Debtors Anonymous is one of several committees designed to serve the Fellowship and work in conjunction with the General Service Board (GSB) and General Service Office (GSO). One member of the GSB also serves as trustee liaison to the PI committee for the purpose of facilitating good communication between the Board, the committee, and the Fellowship.

The WSC Public Information Committee's mandate is to handle all of Debtors Anonymous' national (D.A.) public information responsibilities and to facilitate local and Regional PI Committee work. Some Regions of D.A., local areas, and Intergroups outside the USA have formed their own public information committees, which have the responsibility for facilitating public information in their Region and locally. Public information requests from local media, helping professionals, and all others may be handled best by local PI committees and/or Intergroups. The GSB and the WSC PI Committees also strive to provide experience, strength, and hope to those working at the local level to provide public information.

Contact them at: PublicInfo@debtorsanonymous.org.

WSC PI Statement of Purpose

"The Public Information Committee works to carry the message of D.A. to the still suffering debtor by interacting with the media, helping professionals, the general public, and the D.A. Fellowship at large, in person, on the telephone, and through written information. The Public Information Committee utilizes the Debtors Anonymous Public Information Handbook and other D.A. Service Literature available to the entire D.A. Fellowship as a tool for outreach efforts, supports and trains Regional PI Committees (PICs) and PI Representatives (PIRs) as guided by the Twelve Traditions of Debtors Anonymous."

The WSC Public Information Committee provides information in response to requests from:
1. The general public
2. The media (newspapers, magazines, radio, television, film and internet news outlets)
3. Professionals and institutions – e.g., counselors, therapists, recovery treatment centers, etc.

Its goals are to:

1. Have the ability to RESPOND to public information requests as they come in.
2. Provide information and spread awareness of the availability of Debtors Anonymous where needed.

---

1   For those interested in PI service work, the full text is available as a free download at the D.A. website, www.debtorsanonymous.org/download/public-information-manual/

Regional and local Public Information Committees – responsibilities:

- To read the Twelve Steps, Twelve Traditions, and the Twelve Concepts of Debtors Anonymous to better understand them and how they relate to PI.

- Regional and Local Committees in the USA should contact the GSO in Needham, MA, with all matters pertaining to public information that may have an impact on a national level, at office@debtorsanonymous.org.

- Regional and local PI groups across the world will know best what the Public Information needs and challenges are locally. However, help from the WSC PI Committee or GSB PI Committee, particularly in media training, is available for the asking at PublicInfo@debtorsanonymous.org. Please reach out if you want some help.

- Groups doing PI should notify their Intergroup and let people know what they are doing.

- Regional PI Groups need to answer all inquiries from media, professionals, institutions, and the general public in the local area and/or country and refer all requests from outside of the area to the WSC PI committee or GSB at PublicInfo@debtorsanonymous.org.

- Groups should work with the GSB on any issues needing clarification. Be prepared to respond when notified by the WSC or GSB PI Committees that an action of the GSB may prompt an influx of new inquiries.

Suggested Guidelines for Organizing a Local Public Information Committee

- Meet on a regular basis (at least once a month). Between meetings, have a plan for staying in touch and responding to requests for public information in a timely fashion.

- The committee may consist of 2-3 people; the actual size can be determined by the needs of the local area. At least one person should be from the local Intergroup.

- Have an organized "Tools Packet" from the list of useful tools below.

- The chairperson could send reports of meetings and activities to the GSB PI and WSC PI Committees at PublicInfo@debtorsanonymous.org to keep the flow of information going and to encourage other D.A. members with reports of good news.

Spending Plan for Local Public Information Committees

A spending plan should be prepared quarterly for local or regional public information committees. Each committee determines its own amounts for their spending plan based on the committee's anticipated needs and objectives.

The following are suggested categories for the spending plan:

- Telephone calls

- Postage (responding to inquiries)

- Copying (form letters, meeting lists, etc.)

- Stationery (envelopes)

- Literature (basic D.A. pamphlets)

- Transportation

- Contingency fund

Sample spending plan

Phone calls	$ 5.00
Copies	$ 2.50
Postage (10 stamps/$.50 each)	$ 5.00
Envelopes	$ 2.50
Literature	$ 15.00
Mileage Expense (over 20 miles)	$ 3.50
10 Thumb drives with 3 PSAs plus Welcome Video	$ 12.50
Subtotal	$ 46.00
Contingency Fund (10%)	$ 4.60

Total to be collected each month	**$ 50.60**

Useful Tools for PI Committees

- The Twelve Steps, Twelve Traditions, and Twelve Concepts of Debtors Anonymous

- The Anonymity Statement from the Twelfth Tradition of D.A.

- D.A. Public Information Manual

- D.A. Public Service Announcements available on thumb drives from GSO

- The D.A. PI Starter Kit

- The HIP Starter Kit

- Spending Plan

- Sample Letters as shown under Guidelines for PIRs Responding to Media Requests

- D.A. pamphlet "Debtors Anonymous"

- Your local updated meeting list(s)

- D.A. pamphlet on guidelines for GSRs

- The Fact Sheet on Debtors Anonymous

- D.A. Contact Cards available from the GSO

- Online Literature Order Form

Literature en Español – Spanish

The "home page" of the D.A. website offers several FREE pamphlets en Español (in Spanish). Below are links to the Spanish translations for this free D.A. literature. Download and print some to share with Spanish-speaking newcomers.

Nuestro Propósito is Our Purpose

Unas Palabras para los Recién Llegados is A Word to the Newcomers

Los Doce Pasos de Deudores Anónimos is The Twelve Steps of Debtors Anonymous

Las Doce Tradiciones de Deudores Anónimos is The Twelve Traditions of Debtors Anonymous

Las Doce Herramientas de Deudores Anónimos is The Twelve Tools of Debtors Anonymous

Las Doce Promesas de Deudores Anónimos is The Twelve Promises of Debtors Anonymous

Las Señales de la Deuda Compulsiva is The Signs of Compulsive Debt

Reuniones en Español is Meetings in Spanish

Guidelines for D.A. Members Responding to the Media

Media Training can be made available by the GSB as a conference call for individuals and groups. If your language is not English and you would like training, please contact PublicInfo@ debtorsanonymous.org and the General Service Office and the GSB Committees will work to connect you with interpreters.

The Twelve Traditions of D.A. are our guiding principles in all responses to individuals and organizations outside of the D.A. Fellowship.

Debtors Anonymous exists to help those who suffer from compulsive debting, which is the inability to stop incurring unsecured debt. **Compulsive spending, underearning, and other behaviors can be symptoms of compulsive debting, but are not the primary focus of the D.A. program.**

D.A. members do not give financial advice, but share their experience, strength, and hope as recovering debtors.

Anonymity is a central principle of our Traditions – there should be no television, radio, video, film, or internet appearances, live or recorded, in which the D.A. member is recognizable by name, appearance, or voice.

All inquiries in the USA at the national level should be forwarded to:

Public Information
Debtors Anonymous General Service Office
P.O. Box 920888
Needham, MA 02492
Phone: 781-453-2743 | Toll Free in USA only: 800-421-2382 | Fax: 781-453-2745
PublicInfo@debtorsanonymous.org.

For D.A. outside the USA and for Regional Intergroups and Groups:

If you or your group/meeting has been contacted by the media and wish to respond to it before the next Medial Contact Training, you can email PublicInfo@debtorsanonymous.org or call the General Service Office at (781) 453-2743. Requests in your country may be dealt with by your National or Regional Intergroup who may have experience with local media.

For D.A. Local Groups: If you have an Intergroup in your area, you can make contact with them first. You can also email PublicInfo@debtorsanonymous.org.

When sending materials to professionals, media, and the general public use D.A. Conference-Approved materials or GSB-approved Service Materials from the P.I Manual (also see Useful Tools)

Public Service Announcements (PSAs)

Our Outreach efforts include sharing D.A. PSAs on local TV/Radio stations (including college radio stations) and other institutional-based broadcast systems to ask if they might be interested in airing our PSAs. We share only our experience, strength, and hope. Thumb drives with PSAs and the Welcome Video are available from the GSO. Public Service Announcements for radio, internet sites, and TV stations are available from GSO: office@debtorsanonymous.org.

Requests for a personal interview with a D.A. member or group: Refer to the suggested criteria for D.A. Speakers' Media Interviews on page 11 of the PI Manual as well as the PublicInfo@

debtorsanonymous.org for Media Contact Training.

Suggested Criteria for D.A. Speakers at media Interviews

Who should respond to requests for public information? Members who meet the minimum requirements meet the minimum requirements for being a General Service Representative:

- to be actively working the Twelve Steps

- to have had at least two Pressure Relief Meetings (PRMs)

- to have abstained from incurring new unsecured debt for at least one year

- to have given service to a local group and/or as an Intergroup officer, and to be an active member of a home group

Additionally, they must have completed Media Training. Please contact PublicInfo@ debtorsanonymous.org for information.

N.B.: General Service Board Class B / Non-Debtor Trustees can serve as public faces of D.A. using names and showing faces.

Understanding the Tradition of Attraction versus Promotion

The Fifth Tradition states:

Each group has but one primary purpose—to carry its message to the debtor who still suffers.

The Eleventh Tradition states:

Our public information policy is based in attraction rather than promotion; we need always maintain personal anonymity at the level of press, radio, and film.

Attraction in action: We make D.A. attractive by offering Conference-Approved information about:

- Why we turn to D.A.

- Who we are

- What we are

- What we are not

- Who attends our D.A. meetings

- What happens at our meetings

- What is our Primary Purpose

- The Twelve Promises, which show people what recovery looks like

Recommended Activities for Attracting Members

Here is a list of places to contact in order to spread the word to helping professionals about D.A. and what it offers to the debtor who still suffers. This information is in Spanish as well as in English.

- Consumer Credit Counseling Services

- Bankruptcy Judges/Lawyers, Doctors, CPAs, Accountants, Tax Accountants

- HR Directors and EAPs (Occupational Health) of Corporations

- Counselors: especially Marriage & Family Counselors

- Prisons, Probation Offices, halfway houses

- Retirement Centers/Senior Citizen organizations

- Banks/Credit Unions

- Churches and other places of worship, especially where we meet church and religious leaders

- 24-Hour Crisis Hotlines

- Professional centers

- Newspapers' Self-Help section, community / church / mosque / synagogue, etc. calendars

- Other 12-Step Fellowship meeting centers – put up posters

- TV station / Radio station web pages such as, 'if you have been affected by these issues'

- Hospitals, Recovery Treatment Centers, and Free Clinics

- Teen Centers and Organizations

- Library, grocery store, and Self-Help boards

- Mailing parties – after the D.A. meeting or during, if okay, members of the D.A. fellowship prepare packets for mailing to reach the above

When you contact agencies, such as the ones suggested above, include in your mailing:

- Outreach letters that you can find in the PI Manual

- A sample flyer to post on bulletin boards which includes meeting locations, contact telephone numbers, and the Primary Purpose of D.A.

- A request to have a meeting list published in the organization's calendar of events and with their local, state, and national professional associations

B. Underserved and Under-represented Outreach Recommendation

Whatever your story, you are welcome in Debtors Anonymous. In D.A., we celebrate the rich, diverse experiences of people of all identities. We embrace members of any race, ethnicity, nationality, gender, sexual orientation, age, physical or mental ability, socio-economic status, religious, spiritual, philosophical expression, or any other trait. Our various experiences benefit our recovery, so we encourage all members to value differences and actively participate in making D.A. an inclusive fellowship. Together, we create accessible and welcoming spaces for anyone with the desire to stop incurring unsecured debt, so that we may all recover one day at a time.

Therefore, the UUOC recommends the following guidelines for groups to reach out to the still-suffering debtor in underserved and under-represented communities:

At a meeting, ask: Who is not in this room?

In other words, who in your larger community is not represented or under-represented in the makeup of your D.A. group? You can consider

a. Race, ethnicity, and nationality

b. Gender identity

c. Sexual orientation

d. Age

e. Physical and/or mental abilities

f. Religious, spiritual, or philosophical expression

g. Socio-economic status

h. Language(s) understood and spoken

i. Health and access needs

j. Citizenship status

It may be helpful to look up demographics of your greater geographic area as a guide for understanding who is not represented in your meeting.

For virtual meetings that are less tied to geographic areas, you could consider demographics related to a country, a continent, the globe. If your meeting has a particular focus, consider all the different people who might share that focus.

From here, you can create a list of organizations in your community that serve any of the populations you are looking to reach, such as community centers, places of worship, retirement centers, community colleges, non-profit organizations, etc. Mail a complimentary copy of the D.A. pamphlet "Debtors Anonymous" (currently available in English and Spanish). Provide a cover letter with local contact information and identify D.A. members in recovery who are willing to respond to requests for more information.

Individual members of Debtors Anonymous can also reach out to leaders or individuals in their network who may be in contact with the populations you are looking to reach.

C. Public Information Representative (PIR)

The primary purpose of the Public Information Representative is to carry the message of recovery to the still-suffering debtor and to other people and groups who come in contact with debtors. We seek to be a credible community resource by providing information on D.A. websites and via other communications to the general public, the media, and helping professionals. We also provide information to institutions when there is no local Hospital, Institution, and Prison (HIP) committee. PIRs report to their Intergroup or home group meeting.

Suggested qualifications for a PIR

- Is an active member of Debtors Anonymous, attending meetings regularly with at least three months of not incurring unsecured debt* (*requirement is one year of not incurring unsecured debt for working with the media).

- Has read the Twelve Steps, Twelve Traditions, and Twelve Concepts of Debtors Anonymous, resulting in a firm understanding of anonymity as discussed in Traditions Eleven and Twelve

- Has worked the Steps or is currently engaged in step work with a D.A. sponsor

- Has attended or commits to attending a Media Training workshop

Responsibilities of a PIR

- Report to their home group about PI activities

- Commit to a minimum of one hour per month of service work

- Attend D.A. speaker training and media training within the first year of service

- Be a point person for requests from the media

Suggested activities of a PIR

Public Outreach

In keeping with our 11th Tradition, we spread the word about D.A. to local media (TV, radio, newspapers, Internet sites, etc.). In the USA, we work in cooperation with the World Service Conference (WSC) PI Committee to reach out to professionals and institutions.

Other Regions of D.A. will inform their Intergroup or Regional Intergroup of their PI activities and will exchange ideas with the PIR at that level. We spread the word about D.A., including specific meeting information, to places as suggested above. The PI manual has excellent examples of specific letters, announcements, and meeting listings for these purposes.

In-reach to the D.A. Fellowship

We inform local, regional, and the greater D.A. fellowships about our D.A. activities and events. These include retreats, workshops, meeting anniversary celebrations, days of sharing, etc. We accomplish this by disseminating flyers and notices to other local meetings and Intergroup(s) and by posting notices on D.A.'s eNews. (You can sign up for eNews at http://www.debtorsanonymous. org/)

Resources available to support a PIR

- The Public Information Manual, available as a free download from https://debtorsanonymous. org/download/p-i-manual/?wpdmdl=127542

- The General Service Board of D.A. at:
  Debtors Anonymous General Service Office
  PO Box 920888
  Needham, MA 02492-0009
  Toll Free: 800-421-2383 (U.S. only) | Direct dial: 781-453-2743 | Fax: 781-453-2745
  PublicInfo@debtorsanonymous.org

- The Public Information Starter Kit, available as a free download from https:// debtorsanonymous.org/download/p-i-manual/?wpdmdl=127542

- The HIP Starter Kit, available as a free download from https://debtorsanonymous.org/ download/hip-starter-kit-2/?wpdmdl=68386

- Other PIRs and/or committees at the Intergroup or GSR level

- The World Service Conference PI Committee of Debtors Anonymous

- PI media training sessions

CHAPTER 5 – WORLD SERVICE

A. Debtors Anonymous Conference Structure

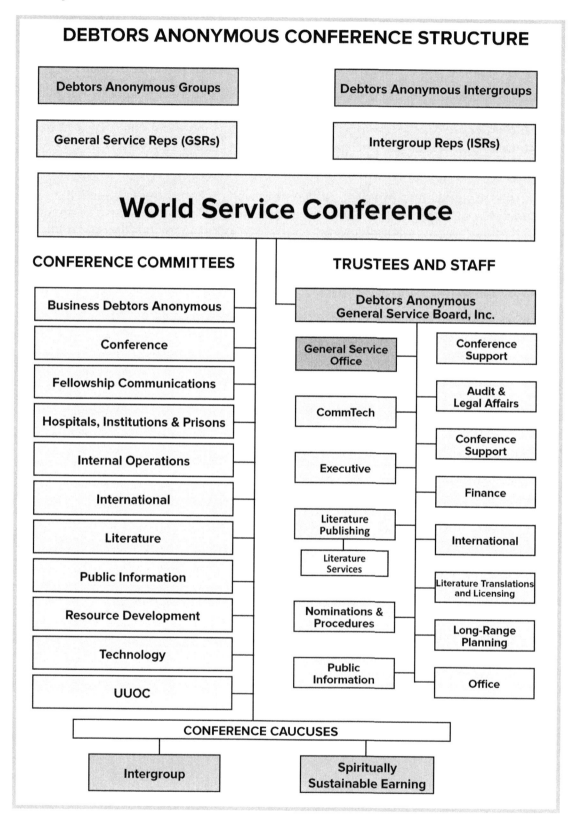

B. The Role of the GSR and ISR
   to the Local D.A. Group, Intergroup, GSR Area Group,
   and the World Service Conference

Service to the Local D.A. Group

The General Service Representative (GSR) is the link between each individual registered D.A. meeting and the World Service Conference (WSC) of Debtors Anonymous. The GSR is an important service position in any D.A. group. It is suggested that a person being considered for GSR have the following qualifications: to have abstained from incurring unsecured debt for at least one year, to be actively working the 12 Steps of D.A., to have a working knowledge of the 12 Traditions, to have had at least two Pressure Relief Meetings, to have given service to a local group, and to be an active member of a home group. It is also helpful if the D.A. member who will take on the job as GSR has successfully completed other service positions at the Intergroup level. In other words, the GSR candidate should be someone the group knows and feels comfortable entrusting with the important task of becoming a member of the World Service Conference of Debtors Anonymous. GSRs help to perform the work needed to support D.A. This is an important commitment for a recovering debtor refraining from debting one day at a time and should be viewed as an ongoing service commitment throughout the following year.

At the conclusion of the World Service Conference, GSRs may wish to reflect on their vision for the future of Debtors Anonymous in their area. GSRs are encouraged to develop an action plan that will encompass continued WSC committee work and encourage participation by D.A. members at the local level. This could include attracting new members, public information work such as mailings or flyers, encouraging others to start groups or Intergroups in areas that do not already have a D.A. presence, and encouraging others to do service.

Service to the Local Intergroup

The Intergroup Service Representative (ISR) also serves as a link between a local Intergroup and the World Service Conference of D.A. The ISR is a voting position created in 1994 by the General Service Conference upon passage of the permanent D.A. Conference Charter. The decision and vote to include ISRs was an important step by the D.A. Fellowship to expand and improve ongoing communication with Intergroups nationwide. The ISR serves the same role as a GSR—to participate on a committee, to vote at the D.A. Convocation, and to become a communication link among all D.A. groups, especially Intergroups.

As a member of the World Service Conference of D.A., the GSR and ISR will be asked to work within the World Service Conference committee structure to serve the interests of D.A. as a whole. GSRs and ISRs are encouraged to stay open to the needs of the Fellowship as a whole, not to only represent the interests of their group or Intergroup.

The GSR, the ISR, and the group representative to the local Intergroup (often called the Intergroup Representative) are separate positions. (The Intergroup Representative attends local Intergroup meetings and represents their home group in matters that affect the geographic area and the

Intergroup's interests. This position is different from the Intergroup Service Representative.) If possible, each position should be held by different people when a group or an area becomes large enough to choose them.

When circumstances warrant, one person may be elected to serve as GSR for several groups when an Intergroup has not been formed; however, a GSR representing more than one group will have only one vote at the Conference, like every other GSR or ISR.

Service to the GSR Area Group

If a GSR Area Group exists, the GSR meets with other GSRs from the region to discuss D.A. issues that affect D.A. as a whole or those that affect the area. If an area group does not exist, the GSR may work with the area Intergroup, which coordinates activities and interests among groups in a close geographical area. As an area grows, groups prosper, and more GSRs are elected, the GSRs are encouraged to form a GSR area group.

Some communities have only one or two meetings, and therefore forming a GSR area group is impractical. It is important, however that groups elect GSRs and, no matter how few or how many meetings there are in the area, GSRs can meet with each other and share their common work of carrying the message. GSRs and ISRs can locate other groups in the area by using the searchable database available online at the D.A. website, www.debtorsanonymous.org.

Service to the World Service Conference

The GSR and ISR assume several responsibilities in assisting the World Service Conference of Debtors Anonymous with ongoing service.

    a. The GSR and ISR (delegates) register their local D.A. group and Intergroup with the General Service Office (GSO). By registering with the GSO, groups are added to the D.A. database. This assures that groups receive newsletters and other communications. It is important that your group information is current.

    b. The delegate represents their group or Intergroup at the annual World Conference as a voting member, communicating the group's needs and opinions about crucial issues affecting the Fellowship. The delegate shares the local "group conscience" with the Conference so that it helps shape the consensus about essential D.A. action plans that the Conference approves.

    c. The delegate participates on a Conference committee of his or her choice, and, if desired, a caucus, and works with that committee and caucus throughout the year to carry out its Conference-approved action steps. (The committees include Business Debtors Anonymous (BDA); Hospitals, Institutions and Prisons (HIP); Fellowship Communications (FCC); Public Information (PI); Literature; Internal Operations (IOC); Conference (CC); Resource Development (RDC); and Technology (Tech). The informal caucuses discuss the concerns of: (1) Intergroups; (2) International; (3) Spiritually Sustainable Earning; and (4) Underserved and Under-represented Outreach.)

    d. The delegate shares the results of the World Service Conference with the local group or Intergroup after the Conference and shares a copy of the WSC Report with the group, which includes the Convocation Minutes—the complete results of the annual business meeting.

    e. The GSR and ISR both have some responsibility for informing the group about the financial needs of the General Service Office and taking some responsibility to promote a timely allocation of the Seventh Tradition when it is collected. The GSR and ISR can encourage the group to adopt a spending plan that takes into account the financial needs of the group, regular contributions to D.A. as a whole, and support the GSR and ISR to attend area meetings and the annual World Service Conference of Debtors Anonymous. The D.A. approved "Meeting Format" recommends the following: "D.A. has a service structure which depends on contributions from our groups. After our group's needs are met, we contribute 45 percent to the General Service Office, 45 percent to Intergroup, and 10 percent to the Area GSR Group."

f. The GSR and an ISR should make every effort to attend the World Service Conference of Debtors Anonymous. Many groups take up regular but separate collections or conduct events to raise adequate funds to send their representatives to the World Service Conference and to area meetings. The John H. Scholarship Fund is available to provide partial assistance to delegates in need.

C. GSR & ISR Qualifications

The Debtors Anonymous World Service Conference (WSC) brings together representatives of D.A.'s registered groups and Intergroups each year to review the state of the Fellowship and make decisions about its future direction. The Conference is an exciting event, and an important one. It gives registered groups and Intergroups throughout the world opportunities to be an integral part of D.A.'s conscience, to participate in the Fellowship's service structure, and to work in close cooperation with the General Service Office and General Service Board of Trustees. But along with those privileges comes responsibility—the responsibility of sending the best-qualified delegates to ensure spiritual decision making and good policies for D.A.'s future. D.A.'s Ninth Concept for World Service states, "Good leaders, together with appropriate measures for choosing them at all levels, are necessary." Nowhere is this more apparent that at the annual WSC.

Long experience has shown that the Conference functions better when the GSRs (General Service Representatives) elected by groups and the ISRs (Intergroup Service Representatives) chosen by Intergroups meet certain qualifications. Most important among those qualifications are to have at least one year of not having incurred any unsecured debt and a successful record of service at the group or Intergroup level. It is also suggested that GSRs and ISRs be actively working the 12 Steps of D.A., have a working knowledge of the 12 Traditions, have had at least two Pressure Relief meetings, and be active in a home group. Furthermore, good GSRs and ISRs have personal qualities that prepare them for the often-challenging work of the Conference—the ability to work in harmony with others, even amid controversy, the stamina to stay focused for long hours during the busiest days of the WSC, and the willingness to follow the spiritual principles by which the Conference operates. Those chosen as delegates should also be aware of the workload—all GSRs and ISRs are expected to work on a standing committee of the Conference for the full length of the WSC, and by telephone or email throughout the year until the next Conference, regardless of when their GSR/ISR term is completed in their individual group or intergroup. They also have the job of carrying the group conscience of their group or Intergroup to the Conference, and of reporting news of the Conference's activities to their groups.

Delegates should be committed to following the spiritual principle of rotation practiced at all levels of the D.A. service structure. GSRs and ISRs, like Trustees and other trusted servants, rotate out of their positions after either one or two 3-year terms, and are expected to serve no more than 3 years on any one committee. Rotation ensures a regular flow of new ideas, and prevents the distraction and disruption caused by a particular individual or issue becoming "entrenched" year after year. The selection of a GSR or ISR is a solemn trust for any D.A. service entity. Members should take the time to find the right person to represent them on the World Service level, and to not allow the selection to become a "personality contest." The strength of the D.A. service structure rests in the group conscience of the GSRs and ISRs who serve our Fellowship at the Conference. D.A. benefits from a strong and unified whole.

—Reprinted from the *DA Focus* April 2007

D. GSR Pamphlet

Text from the GSR pamphlet, reprinted here at the request of the 2003 World Service Conference. All rights reserved. Revisions were made in 2006 and 2008 to update the information.

GSR
General Service Representative

Only through service can we give to others what has so generously been given to us.

– Eleventh Tool of Debtors Anonymous

What Is a GSR?

The General Service Representative (GSR) may be the most important service position in Debtors Anonymous. The GSR is elected by their local group to act as the primary link between the group and the Fellowship as a whole. As GSR, you share with your group up-to-date information from the General Service Office (GSO) and the General Service Board of Trustees (GSB). However, that sharing is only the beginning of a far more interesting—and more rewarding—service role.

What Does a GSR Do?

As a GSR, you have the opportunity to serve your group, your area, the World Conference, and D.A. members around the world in many ways:

Service to Your Group

You not only receive information from the GSO, you also transmit your group's ideas, opinions, and local news to the office and the board. You help all of D.A.'s trusted servants to keep a "finger on the pulse of D.A." With your feedback, the GSO and the GSB can better understand and respond to your group's needs.

- Through you, your group's views become part of the collective conscience of the Fellowship as a whole, as expressed through the will of the annual World Conference.

- After you attend the annual World Conference, you report on the activities and action steps of the Conference to help unify and guide the Fellowship's direction at the local level.

- You share with your group your overall perspective based on the 12 Steps, 12 Traditions, and 12 Concepts of Service that you draw from your experience with other groups and members worldwide.

- Working with your group Treasurer, you remind your group of its responsibility to provide Seventh Tradition support for its area GSR Group, area Intergroup, and the GSB[1] (See Note below.)

- You encourage your group to participate in worldwide D.A. events, such as the annual World Service Month (April) and other special D.A. events at the national and local level.

- You inform your group about D.A. publications and the *Ways & Means*® newsletter and encourage the group to maintain an adequate supply for newcomers and regular members.

- As primary contact, when you are elected, your name, address, and other contact information should be sent to the General Service Office. Mailings for your group from the GSO will be sent to you. (Please include the name of the GSR leaving office to avoid confusion with

---

1   NOTE: The suggested contribution ratio for any surplus funds is 45% to the area Intergroup; 45% to the GSB; and 10% to the Area Group (for fellow GSRs from your region, if any). If there is no Area Group for GSRs, then the suggested ratio is 50% to the Intergroup and 50% to the GSB If there is no Intergroup, then the suggestion is 100% to the GSB. This suggestion was approved by the General Service Board of Trustees in 1989.

changing the registration.)

- You should confirm—once a year—that your group's registration with the GSO is current and the information about meeting locations and times is accurate and up to date.

Service to the World Conference

- You represent your group at the annual World Conference as a voting delegate. You represent your group's needs and its opinions about crucial issues affecting the Fellowship. You share your local "group conscience" with the Conference so that it helps shape the consensus about essential D.A. action plans that the Conference approves.

- You participate on a Conference committee of your choice, and if you so choose, a caucus of your choice, and work with that committee and caucus throughout the year to carry out its Conference-approved action steps. PLEASE NOTE: Delegates are expected to continue their service for the entire duration of the World Service Conference year, regardless of when their term ends at the group or Intergroup level. (The WSC committees include Business Debtors Anonymous (BDA); Hospitals, Institutions and Prisons (HIP); Fellowship Communications (FCC); Public Information (PI); Literature (LIT); Internal Operations (IOC); International (INT); Conference (CC); Resource Development (RDC); Technology (Tech), and Underserved and Under-represented Outreach (UUOC). The informal caucuses discuss the concerns of Intergroups (IG), and Spiritually Sustainable Earning (SSEC).

- You share the results of the World Conference with your local group when you receive a copy of the WSC Report, which includes the Convocation Minutes, the complete results of the annual business meeting.

- NOTE: Each D.A. group is responsible for approving a spending plan that covers the expenses of its GSR—to the extent possible—including attending the World Service Conference.

Service to the Intergroup or Area Group

- If an area GSR group exists, you meet with other GSRs from your region to discuss D.A. issues that affect D.A. as a whole or those that affect your area. If an area group does not exist, you may work with the area Intergroup, which coordinates activities and interests among groups in a close geographical area. As an area grows, groups prosper, and more GSRs are elected, you are encouraged to form a GSR area group.

- Each Intergroup can also elect an ISR who attends the World Service Conference and represents the Intergroup with the same authority and responsibility as a GSR.

- The GSR, the ISR, and the group representative to the local Intergroup are separate positions. If possible, each position should be held by different people when a group or an area becomes large enough to choose them.

- When circumstances warrant, one person may be elected to serve as GSR for several groups when an area Intergroup has not been formed; however, a GSR representing more than one meeting will have only one vote at the Conference like every other GSR or ISR. (A group representative to an Intergroup represents their home group in matters that affect the geographic area and the Intergroup's interests.)

When and How Does a GSR Serve?

- A GSR's term of office is usually three (3) years. A new term should begin before the World Service Conference so that the GSR can serve on a Conference committee during the year after the Conference. It is also suggested that elections be held several months before the new term begins so the new GSR can become acquainted with their duties. Regardless of when a new GSR is elected at the group or Intergroup level, an outgoing GSR is expected to serve at the world level on their committee (and caucus, if applicable) until the end of the Conference year (typically August until that year's WSC).

- A group elects a GSR with the same procedures that it uses for each service position, except that the qualifications may differ.

- Individual groups determine the qualifications for the GSR position. It is suggested that a person being considered for GSR have the following qualifications: to be actively working the 12 Steps, to have had at least two (2) Pressure Relief Meetings (PRMs), to have abstained from incurring new unsecured debt for at least one year, to have given service to a local group and/or as an Intergroup officer, and to be an active member of a home group.

- The group should consider the qualities that make a good D.A. member and a valued trusted servant at any level: patience, tolerance, dedication to the 12 Steps and 12 Traditions, and active support for the D.A. way of life.

- An Alternate GSR should be elected, when possible, to fill in for the GSR as necessary, and to replace the GSR if the GSR is elected to the Board of Trustees.

- It is suggested that a GSR should not hold any other office in your local group or Intergroup. However, it is understood that this may not always be possible in situations where there may be only one or a few D.A. groups and not enough qualified members are available to fill all service positions.

Helpful Information

The following publications may help you better understand the structure and operation of Debtors Anonymous, the World Conference, and the role of a GSR. They are available for purchase from the General Service Office and for free download on the D.A. website:

- Debtors Anonymous Manual for Service

- The Conference Charter of Debtors Anonymous (included in the Service Manual)

- Final Convocation Minutes of the Annual Debtors Anonymous World Service Conference (for the previous year or two)

- The Twelve Concepts of Service in Debtors Anonymous (included in the Service Manual)

- World Meeting Directory of Debtors Anonymous

- General Service Office of Debtors Anonymous pamphlet (included in the Service Manual)

- The Twelve Steps, Twelve Traditions, and Twelve Concepts of Debtors Anonymous

- A Currency of Hope

You may also want to consult the following A.A. materials, available from A.A. meetings or A.A. World Services:

- Twelve Steps and Twelve Traditions

- Alcoholics Anonymous®

- "A.A. Tradition—How It Developed"

Acknowledgments

E. At the World Service Conference of Debtors Anonymous

The GSR and ISR represent their respective group or Intergroup at the annual World Service Conference as a registered voting delegate. The GSR and ISR represent the group's needs and its opinions about crucial issues affecting the Fellowship. The GSR and ISR share the local "group conscience" with the Conference so that it helps shape the consensus about essential D.A. action plans that the Conference approves. Each delegate, however, is entitled to vote according to their own conscience, in the spirit of the Right of Decision described in Concept 3 of the Twelve Concepts for D.A. World Service. The rules and procedures contained in the Twelve Concepts, the Conference Charter, the DAMS, and any special rules of that the Conference may adopt (such as the Literature Approval Process) govern the Conference. To the extent that these rules and procedures do not address an issue, the rules contained in the current edition of Robert's Rules of Order Newly Revised will govern the Conference when they are applicable.

The GSR and ISR share the results of the World Service Conference with their local group when they receive a copy of the World Service Conference Report, which contains the Convocation Minutes—the complete results of the annual business meeting.

Relationship to Conference Committees

As part of their service commitment, GSRs and ISRs are expected to serve on a World Service Conference committee of their choice for the entire conference year. In addition, they also have the option of serving on one of the WSC caucuses.

On the first day of meetings at the Conference, each standing committee and caucus reorganizes for the year, electing a chairperson, vice-chairperson, secretary and treasurer from the registered GSRs and ISRs in attendance. One or more board liaisons elected by the General Service Board are provided access to attend all committee or caucus meeting in order to assist each committee or caucus as a non-voting member.

Many GSRs and ISRs serve on the same committee/caucus for more than one year. While this type of continuity can be beneficial to the Conference, in the spirit of rotation, a motion was passed at the 2007 WSC that, beginning with the 2008 WSC, delegates may serve on the same committee/caucus for a total of no more than three (3) consecutive years with three (3) years off in between.

It's suggested that a GSR/ISR's main role is to listen in the first year, to lead in the second year, and to mentor in the third year. Throughout the service term, GSRs and ISRs get to practice applying program principles to the business of being a delegate at the world level and while working in groups. GSR and ISR service is also a training ground for possible board level service.

It is suggested that upon completion of their Board service, Trustees will refrain from serving as part of the World Service structure again, including the positions of Trustee, Appointed Committee Member (ACM), General Service Representative (GSR), or Intergroup Service Representative (ISR).

However, former Trustees may be invited to serve in a non-voting capacity as special workers or as Project Contributors.

Only registered GSRs and ISRs can vote at WSC committee meetings. All assignments to the prior committee end immediately before the beginning of the new WSC.

Each committee or caucus discusses the issues facing it and prioritizes the items raised during the discussions, using the group conscience process to develop an agenda and an action plan. The committees may also decide to create working subcommittees to help with the workflow. All work undertaken by any subcommittee always returns to the full committee for consideration in the group conscience process.

Committees and caucuses may discuss and act on business carried forward from the previous Conference year, as well as any new issues and concerns within its defined province. However, any motions or recommendations developed in the period between Conferences must be approved by the current year's committee or caucus. WSC committees can make motions at Convocation while caucuses propose recommendations. Caucuses wishing to bring a motion must do so through a WSC committee.

On completion of its discussions, each committee or caucus prepares a report of its work and brings forward any suggested motions or recommendations for consideration at the Convocation. Typically, a draft report is prepared by the chairperson or secretary and circulated for review and comment by the committee's members. The committee or caucus should then formally vote to adopt the final report for presentation at the Convocation.

Each report to be included in the Convocation minutes should be signed by the chair and vice-chair of the committee or caucus before presentation to the Convocation by that committee or caucus chair. It should include a spending plan for the committee or caucus to continue its work by email or telephone conference call during the next twelve months. It is crucial that committee work continue throughout the World Service Conference year. The transition from one Conference year to the next is extremely important to the work of the Conference. The "outgoing" committee should prepare a summary of its work and recommendations for the use of the next year's committee or caucus. On the first night of the Conference, the chairperson (or other representative) from each committee and caucus may be asked to give a brief report to the delegates regarding the work accomplished by their committee or caucus during the preceding year.

The rules and procedures contained in the Twelve Concepts, the Conference Charter, the DAMS, and any special rules of that the Conference may adopt that govern the Conference also govern the Conference committees and caucuses.

F. The World Service Conference Committee and Caucus Structure

There are eleven standing committees and two caucus groups working as the organizational structure of the World Service Conference of Debtors Anonymous.

The WSC Committees

Business Debtors Anonymous Committee (BDA)

Conference Committee (CC)

Fellowship Communications Committee (FCC)

Internal Operations Committee (IOC)

International Committee (INT)

Hospitals, Institutions, and Prisons Committee (HIP)

Literature Committee (LIT)

Public Information Committee (PI)

Resource Development Committee (RDC)

Technology Committee (TECH)

Underserved and Under-Represented Outreach Committee (UUOC)

The WSC Caucuses

Intergroup Caucus (IG)

Spiritually Sustainable Earning Caucus (SSEC)

World Service Conference Committees

BDA COMMITTEE (BDA)

The BDA (Business Debtors Anonymous) Committee's purpose is to carry the message to the still suffering debtor and help them apply the Steps and Traditions to all their affairs and not debt one day at a time. The BDA Committee focuses on issues specific to the needs of D.A. members who own or operate businesses, are self-employed or have a desire to own or operate businesses or be self-employed. The BDA Committee is open to all GSRs and ISRs, not just those who represent BDA groups.

CONFERENCE COMMITTEE (CC)

The Conference Committee is concerned with the general nature of the World Service Conference. This includes:

- The Charter of the World Service Conference and its relationship to the General Service Board and membership of D.A. as a whole

- Issues related to the format of the annual World Service Conference of Debtors Anonymous

- Assistance to the Host Committee in their planning and logistics

- Recommendations of sites for future annual conferences

FELLOWSHIP COMMUNICATIONS COMMITTEE (FCC)

The Fellowship Communications Committee facilitates communication and promotes collaboration among the debtor who still suffers, the Debtors Anonymous membership, the World Service Conference Committees and Caucuses, the General Service Office, and the General Service Board, and oversees Sponsor-A-Group and Promise Six Day. (rev. 2020)

PROMISE SIX DAY is an annual event approved by the 2019 World Service Conference that takes place on the fourth Saturday in April. On this day, members are encouraged to participate in fellowship and to break out of isolation which can be a big part of the disease of debting.

HOSPITALS, INSTITUTIONS, AND PRISONS COMMITTEE (HIP)

The Hospitals, Institutions, and Prisons Committee carries the message of D.A. to the debtor who still suffers within hospital, institution and prison systems.

The Hospitals, Institutions, and Prisons Committee utilizes the Debtors Anonymous HIP Starter Kit and other D.A. Service Literature available to the entire D.A. Fellowship as a tool for outreach efforts and supports and trains HIP representatives as guided by the 12 Traditions of Debtors Anonymous. (rev. 7/17)

INTERNAL OPERATIONS COMMITTEE (IOC)

The primary responsibility of the Internal Operations Committee (IOC) is to support the General Service Office (GSO) of Debtors Anonymous. The committee:

- Focuses on the overall office operations of the General Service Office
- Interacts with the Board Office Liaison and the Office Manager to support the ongoing work of the GSO

INTERNATIONAL COMMITTEE (INT)

The International Caucus became the International Committee in 2019 following a vote by the delegates at the WSC. The International Committee's mission is to exchange information and develop initiatives to support the growth of D.A. internationally.

LITERATURE COMMITTEE (LIT)

D.A. conference-approved literature begins with the Literature Committee. Members participate in all levels of the literature creative process, including:

- Generating ideas for new D.A. literature
- Working closely with members of Literature Services
- Reviewing drafts of literature in process (given to them at the Conference by Literature Services)
- Approving final drafts of D.A. literature
- Bringing motions to approve drafts of literature to Convocation to become conference-approved literature

PUBLIC INFORMATION COMMITTEE (PI)

The Public Information Committee works to carry the message of D.A. to the still suffering debtor by interfacing with the media, helping professionals, the general public and the D.A. Fellowship at large, in person, on the telephone and through written information. The Public Information Committee utilizes the Debtors Anonymous Public Information Manual and other D.A. Service Literature available to the entire D.A. Fellowship as a tool for outreach efforts, and supports and trains PI representatives as guided by the 12 Traditions of Debtors Anonymous.

RESOURCE DEVELOPMENT COMMITTEE (RDC)

Revenue for D.A. is the focus of the Resource Development Committee, including:

- Increasing Seventh Tradition contributions and clarifying the use of Seventh Tradition funds
- Encouraging member participation in service at all levels
- Increasing awareness within the D.A. Fellowship about the importance of self-support (rev. 8/13)

TECHNOLOGY COMMITTEE (TECH)

The Technology Committee is composed of delegates who have experience with and/or interest in leveraging technology to grow D.A. The Tech Committee focuses on harnessing technology to improve access to D.A.'s resources, facilitate communication within D.A. and reach out to the debtor who still suffers. The committee advises the Conference and the GSB, as well as providing hands-on technical expertise where applicable. (rev. 8/13)

UNDERSERVED AND UNDER-REPRESENTED OUTREACH COMMITTEE (UUOC)

The mission of the Underserved and Under-represented Outreach Caucus is to support the Fellowship in carrying the message of Debtors Anonymous to the debtor in underserved populations and locations. We coordinate with World Service Conference committees and caucuses by developing best practices for doing that work and sharing it with D.A. as a whole.

World Service Conference Caucuses

INTERGROUP CAUCUS (IG)

The Intergroup Caucus is composed primarily of ISRs but also includes GSRs and Trustees who have experience with their local Intergroups. The main function of this caucus is to create tools, resources, and a better understanding of the role of an Intergroup in the overall organizational structure of D.A. The Intergroup Caucus helps support both new and existing Intergroups. The Intergroup Caucus also contributes to the efforts to regionalize D.A.

SPIRITUALLY SUSTAINABLE EARNING CAUCUS (SSEC)

The Spiritually Sustainable Earning Caucus (SSEC) serves to support the D.A. Fellowship in gaining clarity around issues of earning in the D.A. program. Our vision is to broaden the Fellowship-wide understanding of how spiritually sustainable earning fits into D.A. recovery, encouraging a comprehensive and spiritual approach by working the Twelve Steps and using the Tools of Debtors Anonymous.

Committee Officers: Chairperson, Vice-Chairperson, Secretary, and Treasurer

The first order of business for each WSC committee and caucus is to elect its officers for the year. It is suggested that a person being considered to serve as the officer of a committee or caucus have the following qualifications: to have abstained from incurring unsecured debt for at least one year, to be actively working the 12 Steps of D.A., to have had at least two Pressure Relief Meetings, to have given service to a local group and/or as an Intergroup officer, and to be an active member of a home group.

THE CHAIRPERSON: Upon election, the chairperson presides over committee meetings, allowing all members to express their opinions. The first responsibility of the chairperson is to create an agenda with returning and new committee members. The chairperson leads the discussion of all agenda items sent to the committee for consideration. The chairperson also facilitates the development of a spending plan, which includes anticipated costs for completing the committee's work, such as telephone calls, postage, copying, and supplies. During the conference, the chairperson also meets with other committee chairs to help the work of Debtors Anonymous.

The chairperson facilitates the work of the committee during the Conference and throughout the following twelve months until the next Conference. The chairperson is responsible for communicating regularly with their General Service Board liaison and writing brief reports for the quarterly service newsletter, the *DA Focus*. All committee or caucus questions, requests, and project proposals should be transmitted by the chairperson through the liaison to the General Service Board to ensure they represent the group conscience of the full committee or caucus. Board approval or feedback may take months, so it is advisable to allow enough time in the conference year. While project proposals and requests must be transmitted by the chairperson to the liaison for board review and approval, any delegate is welcome to reach out to their GSB liaison at any time and for any reason.

On completion of its discussions, each committee and caucus prepares a report of its work, and brings forward any suggested motions or recommendations for consideration at the Convocation. Typically, a draft report is prepared by the chairperson or secretary and circulated for review and comment by the committee's members. The committee or caucus should then formally vote to adopt the final report containing its motions, recommendations, and spending plan before presentation at the Convocation.

Committee and caucus chairpersons are responsible for maintaining a binder, to be passed on to the next chairperson, containing current and past final committee reports, subcommittee reports (or other documents for bringing the incoming committee up to speed on work carried on during the year but not completed), and any other material that would assist the committee in carrying on its work in an effective way.

If a centralized digital repository for all such reports, accessible through DebtorsAnonymous.org, has been developed, that repository is to be used for this purpose. Committees may consider it advisable to maintain a paper copy as well.

THE VICE-CHAIRPERSON: The Vice-Chairperson assumes the responsibilities of the chairperson when the chair is unavailable, both during the World Service Conference and during the year between conferences.

THE SECRETARY: The Secretary of the committee generates a roster of committee participants, including names, addresses, telephone numbers, email addresses, and other contact information where appropriate. It is the Secretary's responsibility to keep the minutes of the meetings as well as to keep track of action items that are to be addressed by the committee during the year.

THE TREASURER: At the Conference, the committee Treasurer will be informed of the amount allocated to the committee by the General Service Board's spending plan. The committee Treasurer will manage the committee's spending plan. Committee members may incur expenses related to their work, such as purchasing literature, copying, postage, and supplies. The committee Treasurer will send a reimbursement form with receipts to the GSB Treasurer, and the GSB Treasurer will reimburse the GSRs.

Committees at the Convocation of the World Service Conference of Debtors Anonymous

Each committee and caucus chairperson will present a written report signed by the officers of the committee/caucus, plus a brief oral report to all the GSRs, ISRs, and General Service Board Trustees attending the World Service Conference Convocation. Each presenter is asked to stay within the allocated time limits at the Convocation. Projection equipment will be made available. Each presentation shall include:

- Recognition of the committee members

- Motions requiring a vote by all GSRs and ISRs in attendance

- Review of the action items the committee plans to address in the upcoming year

- Items that the committee would like guidance and input on from delegates.

- Recommendations to the General Service Board

WHO MAY ATTEND WORLD SERVICE CONFERENCE COMMITTEE MEETINGS?

The work of the World Service Conference (WSC) committees is a formal extension of the Debtors Anonymous World Service Conference, the annual business meeting of the D.A. Fellowship. According to the Conference Charter, only registered delegates who attend the Conference have the right to vote at the Conference. Registered delegates (who attended the last WSC and served as members of a particular committee during the WSC) attend committee phone meetings throughout the remaining Conference year as voting members of that committee.

In 2018, the GSB approved a motion to include a limited exception to the foregoing requirements for GSR/ISR participation on the monthly World Service Conference Committee meetings. The WSC Committee Participation under Extenuating Circumstances policy provides the following exception for a GSR/ISR who did not attend the WSC:

When a registered, returning General Service Representative (GSR) or Intergroup Service Representative (ISR) whose registration fee has been paid, is unable to attend the WSC due to extenuating circumstances that occur within the two-week period preceding the conference, the GSR or ISR may participate as a voting member of a WSC committee during the conference year that follows, provided that: 1) It is the same committee for which they served in the previous conference year, and 2) that the newly formed committee approves the participation of the GSR/ISR.

On rare occasions, a committee may choose to invite a D.A. member who is not a member of the committee to serve as a valuable resource to the committee's deliberations on an ad hoc basis because of their professional expertise or other special skills.* For example, a committee might choose to invite a guest who has key information to help it with a project. Any such person would attend a meeting as a guest of the committee, without voting privileges, and should not participate in any other way as a committee member unless agreed to in advance by a vote of the committee. For example, a committee might vote to allow such person to attend a single meeting, but not others; or for only a portion of a meeting, etc. Any decision to invite a guest is made by a vote of the committee. The discussion and vote should be done before the potential guest is extended an invitation to join the committee and the potential guest should not be present for the committee's discussion and vote about the guest's presence.

Because the presence of guests may be distracting to some committee members or disruptive to a committee's workflow, a committee should not invite a non-member to attend without advance notice and a unanimous vote to do so. If even one member objects, the committee, in the spirit of Unity, should respect and strongly consider this minority opinion in its deliberations.

D.A. members who wish to serve on a WSC committee are encouraged to do so through the normal process; become a GSR for your group or an ISR for your Intergroup. Since every group is autonomous and should be fully self-supporting through its own contributions, it is up to the group conscience to decide whether they will fully support their representative's expenses to the WSC. John H. scholarship has supported many GSRs and ISRs to attend the WSC each year.

*GSB Project Contributors apply for service to work on special projects the GSB level. At times, a GSB Project Contributor may work with a WSC committee or caucus as part of a special project for a length of time to be determined by the GSB committee to which they are assigned. Any WSC committee or caucus request need to go through their GSB Liaison for approval according to the standard approval process.

WSC Committee and Caucus Motion Approval Process

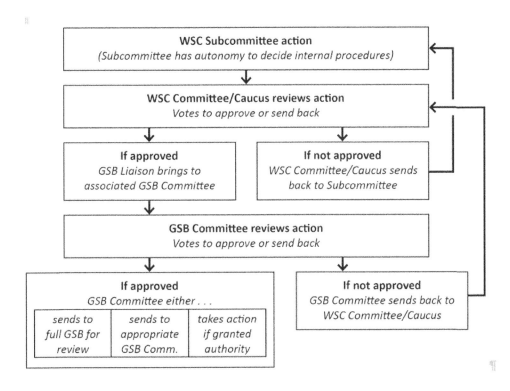

Motions that affect D.A. as a whole are typically reviewed and approved by various WSC and GSB committees and subcommittees before implementation. Procedural motions (for example, meeting times, meeting agenda and minutes) are exempt from this process but main motions (for example, flyers, events, surveys, service literature, Fellowship-wide calls, project proposals, outside communications, etc.) all go through the approval process as follows:

- A WSC committee or subcommittees approves a motion. Note that WSC subcommittees must bring their approved motions before the full committee or caucus for a vote.

- Upon approval at the WSC committee or caucus level, the Chair sends the approved motion and any accompanying documents or proposals to their GSB Liaison for review and/or approval by their associated GSB committee (see list below).

- Upon approval by the associated GSB committee, the motion is either implemented or forwarded to the full GSB or appropriate GSB committee for review and/or approval. (See flow chart above).

- If not approved at a level, the motion returns to the previous level for review and possible revision.

List of WSC Committees/Caucuses and their associated GSB Committees

WSC BDA Committee —> GSB Literature Publications Committee

WSC Conference Committee —> GSB Conference Support Committee

WSC Fellowship Communications Committee—> GSB Communications and Technology Committee

WSC HIP Committee —> GSB Public Information Committee

WSC Internal Operations Committee —> GSB Office Committee

WSC International Committee —> GSB International Committee

WSC Literature Committee —> GSB Literature Publications Committee

WSC Public Information Committee —> GSB Public Information Committee

WSC Resource Development Committee —> GSB Finance Committee

WSC Technology Committee —> GSB Communications and Technology Committee

WSC Intergroup Caucus —> GSB Office Committee

WSC Spiritually Sustainable Earning Caucus —> GSB Literature Publications Committee

WSC Underserved and Under-represented Outreach Caucus —> GSB Public Information Committee

G. Distribution of Flyers at the WSC [2]

If the material for a proposed flyer/announcement ("the material"):
    a. Is the text of a motion or recommendation that a committee (or a recommendation

---

2   Approved by D.A. GSB 8/2010

that a caucus) will present at the Convocation, that the material be submitted to the caucus'/committee's GSB liaison for review, and when approved by the GSB Chair, after consultation with the Parliamentarian, it may be distributed to Conference delegates in the Convocation hall.

b. Relates to a committee's service activities and is not the text of a committee's motion or recommendation, that the material be submitted to the committee's GSB liaison for review and decision. The liaison may choose, for legal, financial, or Traditions implications, to refer the material to the GSB for further review and decision before the material is distributed to the Conference delegates. Material will be displayed in a location which shall be designated by the GSB for Conference-related flyers/announcements. The location will be outside the Convocation hall.

c. Is not related to either a committee's motion or recommendation nor is related to a committee's service activities, a delegate or group of delegates can display a flyer/ announcement that will be available to other Conference delegates; such flyers/ announcements shall be displayed only in the Hospitality Room.

This category of material should be related to Fellowship activities and is distinct from personal communications, which should be placed on the message board made available at the WSC. These flyers cannot contain announcements about events which pose a time conflict with WSC business. Also, these flyers/announcements cannot contain inappropriate, personal, or commercial solicitations.

H. Research and Survey Guidelines for Debtors Anonymous

As D.A. continues to grow as a recovery fellowship, it is important for those who serve on a World Service Conference committee or caucus to keep the needs of individual D.A. members and groups at the forefront of our consideration. Member and group research can be a valuable tool to help accomplish that goal, but we must remain always mindful of the 12 Traditions of D.A. when information is requested and shared. Care should especially be taken to observe the following Traditions:

Tradition 10.

D.A. has no opinion on outside issues; hence the D.A. name ought never be drawn into public controversy.

Application: Examples of outside issues include legal, medical and financial advice, as well as politics, religion, work and professional affiliations, other 12 step fellowships and psychotherapy. In keeping with Tradition 10, a D.A. fellowship research study should avoid asking questions about these areas, for example, "Have you taken bankruptcy?" or "What is your occupation?" By reporting responses to questions dealing with outside issues, the originator of the survey could be presenting information that implies tacit approval by D.A.; thus, this line of questioning should be avoided.

Tradition 12.

Anonymity is the spiritual foundation of all our Traditions, ever reminding us to place principles before personalities.

Application: Precautions ought to be taken to protect the anonymity of survey respondents in paper or on-line research by not requesting the name, email address, or other contact information from the respondent. In the case of paper surveys, respondents should be instructed not to provide contact information and to avoid writing their name and return address on the survey return envelope. For online surveys, the survey should be conducted using a service that does not collect email address information from respondents. Surveys or links that are emailed should place members' email addresses in the "bcc" address row, so that survey recipients are not able to see each other's email addresses.

Group Research: When a WSC Committee conducts research at the group level through a single point of contact such as a GSR, instruct the group not to collect and report any information that would allow individual members to be identified. Special care must be taken with D.A. members' contact information; the use of e-mail addresses and phone numbers ought never to be used for any form of solicitation or private enterprise.

Using the Traditions: It is suggested that the instructions to the survey include the language from Traditions 10 & 12, as well as an explanation of what the information gathered will be used for, how the results will be communicated and contact information for survey recipients to ask questions or register concerns. It is important to err on the side of caution when surveying D.A. members to maintain the spiritual health of our Fellowship. GSB liaisons to WSC committees are a good source of guidance in this regard.

Prepared by the 2013-14 Fellowship Communications Committee
Approved by the GSB June 22, 2014

I. Approval Process for Events and Proposals at the World Level

WSC Committees and Caucuses and GSB Committees have the opportunity to submit proposals to host Fellowship-wide events at the world level of D.A., which may be published on the D.A. website, in eNews announcements to the mailing list, in the *Ways & Means* magazine, and/or the *DA Focus* service newsletter, all of which are managed by the General Service Board. Events that originate at the Intergroup, regional, or meeting level are best promoted locally and are not announced at the world level. Currently videoconference events are not allowed at the world level to insure anonymity, as well as other reasons. The only exceptions are Promise Six Day and the New Year's Meeting Marathon that starts off D.A. International Month, both of which were approved by the World Service Conference.

The GSB looks at several factors when approving proposals, such as the Twelve Traditions, logistical capability, and precedent set by other 12-step fellowships. There can be a 2-month turnaround for approval, which involves adding to a GSB committee agenda, discussion, and vote, and adding to the GSB agenda, discussion, and vote.

FELLOWSHIP-WIDE CALLS

WSC Committees and Caucuses and GSB Committees have the opportunity to host Fellowship-wide calls throughout the year on topics related to their mission. The calls must adhere to the Traditions and be appropriate for publication on the D.A. website. Audio recordings will be published to the website unless members submit complaints. The GSB reserves the right to not publish recordings or approve events.

GSB approval for a call can sometimes take more than one month, so planning ahead is essential.
1. When the WSC Committee or Caucus votes in favor of the motion for the call, a request for Board approval is submitted to their GSB Liaison.
    a. The request should be in the form of a proposal, which should include the call title, a sub-title, a short description of the topic and purpose, and three possible dates and times for the call. (Members can visit the D.A. website Events page to view the calendar with potential available dates.)
    b. A non-color flier for the eNews announcements should also be submitted (in an editable Word document).
    c. The above materials are then submitted through the GSB Liaison to the relevant GSB committee.
2. The GSB Committee, and the GSB if necessary, vote to approve the call. The Board liaison will inform the Committee or Caucus and will send the information to the GSB Technology and Communications Committee for listing on the Events page of the D.A. website.

3. The GSB Liaison will notify the WSC Committee or Caucus if the topic for the call has been approved. If adjustments are needed, the GSB Liaison will endeavor to outline what changes the GSB suggests.

J. Regional Forums

In December 2009, D.A. held its first Regional Forum in Boston pursuant to the recommendation of the 2008 Regionalization Study Commission that read as follows:

We do believe that the two-pronged educational approach suggested by last year's commission will help build the ranks of qualified trusted servants. Such an approach would involve the participation of the General Service Office (GSO), the GSB and Intergroups in creating workshops on the Steps, Traditions and service opportunities on the local, regional, national and international level. Funding, planning and staffing the workshops would be a joint effort of the GSB and Intergroups.

This was followed by a second Forum in Minneapolis and a third in Los Angeles, both in 2010.

The purpose of a Regional Forum is to help develop a culture of service within D.A. This is accomplished by working in tandem with a local Intergroup to present a day-long workshop for members of D.A. focusing in on selected issues or topics. Among the issues discussed are the work and finances of the General Service Board (GSB), the process by which D.A. literature is developed, the General Service Office (GSO), the history of D.A., and the D.A. Archives. In addition, Intergroup participants present a discussion of opportunities for service on the Intergroup level and all participants share in a discussion of the importance of the 12 Traditions to personal recovery.

Forums present an opportunity for D.A. members to interact with members of the GSB and to seek answers to questions they may have. They also provide a chance for members of D.A. to present suggestions to the GSB and to interact with Board members in formulating future goals for D.A. In addition, they give the Board members an occasion to meet with individual members and Intergroup officers and representatives to learn more of the problems and difficulties facing each part of the Fellowship.

An important aspect of each Forum is the opportunity for extensive questions and answers after each presentation. At least three Trustees are in attendance and every effort is made to ensure that all inquiries are answered fully. If an Intergroup makes a request, it may be possible to have one Trustee remain for a second day to participate in an Intergroup funded and scheduled event.

Forums are planned for each year, with ongoing supervision and coordination by the Long Range Planning Committee of the GSB. In order to bring this information on service to as widespread and diverse an audience as possible, different cities will be chosen to host each Forum over the first four years of operation. The Board hopes to hold Forums in every area of the United States during this period. While finances do not presently permit a Forum outside the United States—this is a long-term goal.

The workshop on the Traditions is of particular importance. All too often in the process of recovery, the Traditions are relegated to a "back burner." This workshop seeks to introduce the D.A. member to the idea that the Traditions can play an important role in the process of recovery. As we learn to apply the Traditions to our lives in D.A. service, we can see how they can apply to all our affairs and help us to improve our personal relationships with all people in our lives.

The Intergroup workshop can help the member new to service to understand how she or he can help carry the message to the still-suffering debtor locally. It can also help the Intergroup by providing exposure to those with experience in Intergroup service from outside the immediate area. Finally, this workshop can help attune the GSB to the needs of local Intergroups and start an exploration of ways in which the GSO, the GSB, and the Intergroups can provide support for each other in carrying the message.

The Report of the GSB Chair or Treasurer presents an opportunity to learn what is done with the monies so generously contributed by groups and individuals to the GSB. There will be a review of D.A.'s budget and an overview of the Five-Year Plan for D.A. adopted at the 2009 WSC. There will be discussion of our efforts to implement this Plan and our efforts to develop a new Plan for the next five-year period. The presentation on D.A. history, the Archives, and the GSO afford members an opportunity to learn how they can most effectively use the services that D.A. provides its members. They can also learn about how they can help the operations of GSO as volunteers, even though they may be located at a distance from the Office.

The workshop on literature provides an explanation of the process outlined in this Manual. Members will discover how their ideas or desires for new literature or for revision of existing materials may be realized. We provide clarification for what is for many members an unfamiliar procedure, and give further information on trademark, copyright, and other intellectual property issues facing D.A.

In short, Regional Forums provide an opportunity for growth to an informed and concerned D.A. member and participant in service. They bring the distant Office to the local member. They acquaint the membership with the Board. They help those who have concerns for D.A. to express those concerns effectively and they help all participants—Trustees, Intergroups and members—to learn about each other and how they may work together to carry out D.A.'s primary purpose.

K. The Conference Charter of Debtors Anonymous [3]

1. **Purpose:** The General Service Conference of Debtors Anonymous (D.A.) is the guardian of the world services and the Twelve Steps and Twelve Traditions of Debtors Anonymous and addresses matters affecting Debtors Anonymous as a whole. The Conference shall be a service body only never a government of Debtors Anonymous.

2. **Composition of Conference:** The body of voting delegates is composed of the following who desire to participate: the Trustees of the General Service Board, the selected General Service Representatives of all registered Debtors Anonymous groups, and a representative of each Intergroup registered with the General Service Office. A collection of groups may choose to elect a single General Service Representative to represent the collection, provided the General Service Representative is approved by all groups in the collection. Such General Service Representative will still only receive one vote at the Conference.

3. **Conference Relation to D.A.:** The Conference will act for Debtors Anonymous in the perpetuation and guidance of its world services, and it will also be a vehicle by which the Debtors Anonymous movement can express its view up on all matters of vital Debtors Anonymous policy and all hazardous deviations from Debtors Anonymous Traditions. Conference members should be free to vote as their conscience dictates, they should also be free to decide what questions should be taken to the group level, whether for information, discussion, or their own direct instruction. No change in Article Ten (10) of the Charter or in the Twelve Traditions of Debtors Anonymous or in the Twelve Steps of Debtors Anonymous may be made with less than the written consent of three-quarters (3/4) of the Debtors Anonymous groups.

4. **Conference Relation to the General Service Board:** The Conference functions as guides and advisors to the General Service Board (GSB) and General Service Office (GSO). The General Service Board will consult the Conference on all matters affecting Debtors Anonymous as a whole. The Conference will be expected to afford a reliable cross section of Debtors Anonymous opinion for this purpose.

   A quorum shall consist of two-thirds (2/3) of all the Conference members registered at the annual meeting.

   It will be understood, as a matter of tradition, that a two-thirds (2/3) vote of the Conference members voting shall be considered binding upon the General Service Board and its

---

3   Adopted by the Conference September 1994, revised August 2003, August 2006, August 2007, August 2017

related corporate services, provided the total vote constitutes at least a Conference quorum.

No such vote ought to impair the legal rights of the General Service Board to conduct business and make ordinary contracts relating thereto.

It will be further understood regardless of the legal prerogatives of the General Service Board, as a matter of tradition, that a three-quarter (3/4) vote of all Conference members present may bring about a reorganization of the General Service Board and staff members of the General Service Office, if or when such reorganization is deemed essential.

Under such proceeding, the Conference may request resignations, may nominate new Trustees, and may make all necessary arrangements regardless of the legal prerogative of the General Service Board.

5. **Term of Office for Group Service Representatives:** The recommended term of office for a General Service Representative shall be three years duration, up to two terms.

6. **The General Service Conference Meetings:** The Conference will meet yearly in a location selected by the Conference. The Conference may adopt a policy permitting some or all otherwise-eligible delegates who are unable to attend in person to participate remotely. The Board, in implementing the policy, may modify it if necessary to ensure its effectiveness. The site of the annual meeting will be selected yearly, at least two years in advance. Special meetings may be called should there be a grave emergency. The Conference may render advisory opinions at any time by mail, email, or telephone poll in aid of the General Service Board or its related services.

7. **The General Service Board; Composition, Jurisdiction, Responsibilities:** The General Service Board of Debtors Anonymous shall be an incorporated trusteeship, composed of debtors and non-debtors who elect their own successors, soliciting nominations from all interested parties when a vacancy occurs. These choices are subject to the approval of the Conference or a committee thereof. Interim Board members elected between Conference meetings will start terms immediately and will be subject to approval at the next annual Conference meeting.

    The General Service Board is the chief service arm of the Conference, and is essentially custodial in its character. The General Service Board shall make an annual report of its activities, finances, and current membership.

    Except for decisions upon matters of policy, finance, or Debtors Anonymous Traditions liable to seriously affect Debtors Anonymous as a whole, the General Service Board has complete freedom of action in the routine conduct of policy and business affairs of the Debtors Anonymous service corporations and may name suitable committees and elect directors in pursuance of this purpose.

    Except in great emergency, neither the General Service Board nor any of its related services ought to ever take any action liable to greatly affect Debtors Anonymous as a whole without first consulting the Conference. It is nevertheless understood that the Board shall at times reserve the right to decide which of its actions or decisions may require the approval of the Conference.

8. **The General Service Conference, in General Procedures:** The Conference will hear the financial and policy reports of the General Service Board. The Conference will advise the trustees and staff members upon all matters presented as affecting Debtors Anonymous as a whole, engage in debate, appoint necessary committees, and pass suitable resolutions for the advice or direction of the General Service Board and its related services.

    The Conference may also discuss and recommend appropriate action respecting serious deviations from Debtors Anonymous Traditions or harmful misuse of the name "Debtors Anonymous."

    The Conference may draft any needed bylaws and will name its own officers and committees by any method of its own choosing.

At the close of each yearly session, the Conference will draft a full report of its proceedings, to be supplied to all General Service Representatives, and a condensation thereof will be sent to Debtors Anonymous groups throughout the world.

9. **Amendment to the Conference Charter:** The Conference Charter stands as the principal document defining the relationships between the General Service Conference and Debtors Anonymous as a whole. Amendment of this Charter should be made with great deliberation and forethought. Amendment of the Conference Charter will require that the text of such amendment be sent to the General Service Representatives of all registered groups and to all registered Intergroups, postmarked one hundred and twenty (120) days prior to the first day of the annual meeting of the Conference. Only a voting member of the Conference can move to make such an amendment. At the annual meeting, three-quarters (3/4) of all voting Conference members present will be required to pass the amendment, provided this vote constitutes at least a Conference quorum.

10. **General Warranties of the Conference:** In all its proceedings, the General Service Conference shall observe the spirit of Debtors Anonymous Traditions, taking great care that the Conference never becomes the seat of perilous wealth or power; that sufficient operating funds, plus an ample reserve, be its prudent financial principle; that none of the Conference members shall ever be placed in a position of unqualified authority over any of the others; that all important decisions be reached by discussion, vote, and whenever possible by substantial unanimity; that no Conference action ever be personally punitive or an incitement to public controversy; that though the Conference may act for the service of Debtors Anonymous, it shall never perform any acts of government; and that, like the Society of Debtors Anonymous which it serves, the Conference itself will always remain democratic in thought and action.

The Conference Charter is the principal document of communication between the General Service Representatives, Intergroups, and the General Service Board.

CHAPTER 6 – APPOINTED COMMITTEE MEMBERS

A. Frequently Asked Questions about Becoming an Appointed Committee Member to the Debtors Anonymous General Service Board [4]

What is the Debtors Anonymous General Service Board?

The Debtors Anonymous General Service Board, Inc. (D.A. GSB) is a 501(c)(3) not-for-profit organization incorporated in the State of New York. The General Service Board is the chief service arm of the D.A. World Service Conference and is essentially custodial in its character.

What is an Appointed Committee Member?

Each committee of the General Service Board may choose to select one or more Appointed Committee Members (ACMs) to serve on the committee. These ACMs are recovering D.A. members who usually have needed experience or expertise in a particular field, such as computer technology, literature development, or public relations.

How are ACMs chosen?

Suggestions for candidates are sought from any GSB Trustee, GSR, ISR, Board Committee, Conference Committee (including the Convocation), GSR Group, Intergroup, D.A. group, or D.A. member. Resumes are reviewed by the GSB committee, placing emphasis on the candidate's D.A. recovery, special qualifications, service experience, and dedication to D.A. service. Eligible candidates are interviewed by the committee. A candidate for ACM is elected if he or she receives a unanimous vote of the GSB committee members present and voting, provided a quorum is present, followed by a vote of at least two-thirds of the members of the full General Service Board who are present and voting, provided that a quorum is present. Should the ACM wish to renew their service for a second three-year term, a unanimous vote of the GSB committee they serve on, and a two-thirds vote of the entire GSB in attendance and voting would again be required. ACM contact information is forwarded to the GSB Nominations Committee to keep on file as possible future candidates for GSB Trustee.

What do ACMs do?

ACMs meet via teleconference with the Trustee members of the committee on which they serve. As members of the committee, they are able to generate and vote on motions, make suggestions, and participate in all aspects of the work of the particular committee. ACMs are not members of the General Service Board and therefore do not participate in GSB conference calls. However, ACMs may be invited to meet with the GSB at one of the annual face-to-face business meetings.

How long do ACMs serve?

ACMs serve for a three-year term, renewed on a yearly basis, for a maximum of two three-year terms.

What are the suggested qualifications to become an ACM?

The General Service Board of Debtors Anonymous has found that the same attributes that denote effective Trustees are also those that contribute most towards being able to fulfill a General Service Board Appointed Committee Member commitment. It is suggested that an ACM nominee would:

1. Be a member of D.A. who regularly attends meetings, has a sponsor and is a sponsor, has and sits on Pressure Relief Groups, and has at least three years of not incurring any new unsecured debt.

---

4   Revised, February 2012.

2. Be committed to working the 12 Steps of D.A.

3. Be committed to service as a principle of life; have a willingness and desire to grow through service with the knowledge that it will have its challenges, requires a definite commitment of time, and that world service takes priority over other service.

4. Be dedicated to and active in D.A. service, as demonstrated by successful completion of service commitments on an ongoing basis.

5. Have the ability to follow through with commitments and show willingness to complete the commitment in accordance with D.A. principles, D.A. Tools, the 12 Steps and the 12 Traditions.

6. Have a desire and the ability to perform leadership roles in the spirit of being a trusted servant rather than a ruler and have the ability to work independently while at the same time being part of a team.

7. Be dedicated and committed to the health of D.A. and have a desire to carry the message to the still-suffering debtor.

8. Understand the difference between majority rule and group conscience and be willing to work within the group conscience.

9. Have a flexible attitude and the ability to work with other people even if the direction was not the first choice.

10. Have reliable and private access to a telephone, a computer, a printer, and email.

11. Have effective communication skills, including the ability to listen to others and speak honestly, the ability to write and deliver reports, the ability to follow up on messages and engage in the group process with the members of the GSB committee, and the ability to use the telephone, email, and the Internet.

12. Have good time management and organizational skills.

13. Have the ability to travel once a year on GSB business when/if necessary (see policy below).

14. Have the willingness to use one's full name, address, telephone number, and email address in order to communicate effectively with the GSB and the General Service Office.

How do I nominate someone or myself for GSB ACM?

A nomination consists of three items:
1. **A Signed Letter of Intent:** This is a signed letter from the nominee stating their interest in serving on a particular GSB committee and that he or she meets the guidelines as described above. Please be sure to include all contact information, including full name, address, telephone number, and email address.

2. **A Service Resume:** A resume/biography of the nominee showing prior D.A. service, other 12-step service, and any qualifications or experience that may be helpful to the GSB committee.

3. **A Signed Letter of Recommendation:** A signed letter from the nominating person or group making the nomination and stating their knowledge of the nominee's D.A. recovery and experience in a service role or activity.

What form should the nomination package take?

The three items in the nomination package need to be either mailed or sent electronically (ideally be emailed as an attachment in Word, rtf, pdf, or jpg formats) to:

GSB Nominations Committee
c/o the General Service Office
PO Box 920888

Needham, MA 02492-0009
office@debtorsanonymous.org

Who can nominate a candidate?

Any GSB Trustee, GSR, ISR, Board Committee, Conference Committee (including the Convocation), GSR Group, Intergroup, D.A. group, D.A. member, or collection thereof may nominate a recovering debtor for ACM service.

What is the deadline for submitting a nomination?

New ACMs may start at any time during the year, based on approval by the GSB Committee and the entire Board, requiring no official ratification at the annual World Service Conference.

How will I be notified if my nomination has been approved?

The chairperson of the GSB Committee will notify the candidate of the outcome of the committee review process by email or mailed letter to the address given by the candidate. Newly elected ACMs will be expected to rotate off other world-service level commitments as soon as they are confirmed as ACMs.

What happens if my nomination is not approved?

The GSB committee reviews each candidate's qualifications very carefully. The review process may include interviewing a candidate by telephone and/or email. In general, GSB committees look for candidates who have a history of strong D.A. recovery, consistent and effective D.A. service, a willingness to serve D.A. as a whole, and the ability to work well in the context of the spiritual group conscience process, as well as expertise in the committee's area. Sometimes, after reviewing a candidate's service history, the GSB committee may decline to approve a nomination. In some cases, a GSB committee may decide not to seek the assistance of an ACM. Some areas of D.A. service handled by the General Service Board may not be suitable for the participation of ACMs, for example, areas where D.A. employees' or Trustees' personal information may be involved. Contact the GSB Committee chairperson to determine if there are other ways to be of service to the committee.

What is the travel policy for ACMs?

Appointed Committee Members do not usually attend either the annual D.A. World Service Conference or the General Service Board's annual Face to Face (F2F) business meeting. However, the special talents and abilities of ACMs are sometimes helpful at these events. The GSB will reimburse for travel and related expenses to the WSC or F2F by ACMs provided the committee can produce compelling evidence to the full GSB that the benefit of having the ACM there in person is worth the cost of travel. Such requests will be voted on by the GSB on a case-by-case basis.

B. Additional Information about ACM Service on the Literature Services Board

Following are the suggested guidelines for the Literature Services Board:

Members:
1. Are appointed by the General Service Board
2. Consists of 3-6 members
3. Will include at least one General Service Board Trustee
4. The GSB Trustee may serve as Chair
5. Will meet regularly during the year via teleconference to assure that:
    a. All new literature is created in a prompt, efficient manner

      b. Each new piece carries the D.A. message with a focus on the 12 Steps and/or 12 Traditions as the foundation to recovery from compulsive debting

6. Serve for 3 years, renewed on a yearly basis, for a maximum of two 3-year terms.

Functions:

1. Implements the Literature Approval Process
2. Receives ideas for literature that are generated by the World Service Conference Literature Committee
3. Creates D.A. literature (writing, hiring/managing subcontracted writers)
4. Edits D.A. literature (works in progress, revising/updating existing literature)
5. Reports quarterly to the GSB and annually to the World Service Conference on the current status of literature

CHAPTER 7 – PROJECT CONTRIBUTORS

GSB Project Contributors

A new service opportunity, GSB Project Contributor, was developed and initiated by the GSB in 2018. It provides an opportunity for a member to participate in service to a GSB Committee on a specific task or project, for a shorter time commitment than an ACM, generally for a term of approximately 3-9 months. Former D.A. Trustees are eligible to apply to serve as GSB Project Contributors one year following completion of their GSB service.

Members can apply for a specific project or may offer their availability for service to the Nominations Committee, who will then connect with the member to assess where their skills and interest may be useful to a specific GSB committee.

Once approved and assigned to a GSB Committee, they are eligible to attend that committee's monthly meetings as a non-voting member, although attendance is not required. Depending on the scope of the project, the GSB Project Contributor may also interact with one or more WSC committees or caucuses with all project requests being referred to their GSB liaison.

As the concept of GSB Project Contributor develops and evolves, GSB committees are identifying areas of need and have been making announcements via eNews regarding opportunities to serve those committees.

What are the suggested qualifications to become a GSB Project Contributor?

The General Service Board of Debtors Anonymous has found that the same attributes that denote effective Trustees and/or ACMs are also those that contribute most towards being able to fulfill a General Service Board Project Contributor commitment. It is suggested that a GSB Project Contributor nominee would:

1. Be a member of D.A. who regularly attends meetings, has a sponsor and is a sponsor, has and sits on Pressure Relief Groups, and has at least three years of not incurring any new unsecured debt.
2. Be committed to working the 12 Steps of D.A.
3. Be committed to service as a principle of life; have a willingness and desire to grow through service with the knowledge that it will have its challenges, requires a definite commitment of time, and that world service takes priority over other service.
4. Be dedicated to and active in D.A. service, as demonstrated by successful completion of service commitments on an ongoing basis.
5. Have the ability to follow through with commitments and show willingness to complete the commitment in accordance with D.A. principles, D.A. Tools, the 12 Steps and the 12 Traditions.
6. Have a desire and the ability to perform leadership roles in the spirit of being a trusted servant rather than a ruler and have the ability to work independently while at the same time being part of a team.
7. Be dedicated and committed to the health of D.A. and have a desire to carry the message to the still-suffering debtor.
8. Understand the difference between majority rule and group conscience and be willing to work within the group conscience.
9. Have a flexible attitude and the ability to work with other people even if the direction was not the first choice.
10. Have reliable and private access to a telephone, a computer, a printer, and email.
11. Have effective communication skills, including the ability to listen to others and speak honestly, the ability to write and deliver reports, the ability to follow up on messages and

engage in the group process with the members of the GSB committee, and the ability to use the telephone, email, and the Internet.

12. Have good time management and organizational skills.

13. Have the willingness to use one's full name, address, telephone number, and email address in order to communicate effectively with the GSB and the General Service Office.

How do I nominate someone or myself for GSB Project Contributor?

A nomination consists of three items:

1. A Signed Letter of Intent: This is a signed letter from the nominee stating their interest in serving on a particular GSB committee and that they meet the guidelines as described above. Please be sure to include all contact information, including full name, address, telephone number, and email address.

2. A Service Resume: A resume/biography of the nominee showing prior D.A. service, other 12-step service, and any qualifications or experience that may be helpful to the GSB committee.

3. A Signed Letter of Recommendation: A signed letter from the nominating person or group making the nomination and stating their knowledge of the nominee's D.A. recovery and experience in a service role or activity.

What form should the nomination package take?

The three items in the nomination package should be sent electronically (ideally be emailed as an attachment in Word or pdf format) to:

office@debtorsanonymous.org

CHAPTER 8 – D.A. LITERATURE

A. Conference-Approved Literature

Conference-approved literature is an essential and crucial way to ensure the integrity of the D.A. Program. Tradition One states:

Our common welfare should come first; personal recovery depends upon D.A. unity.

It is not the purpose of D.A. to acquaint its members with all the approaches to the problem of compulsive debting—only the D.A. approach. Conference-approved literature keeps the focus on our spiritual message. As our Program grows, we each benefit in many ways. We are able to attend meetings anywhere in the world, knowing that the D.A. message of hope and help will be consistent and uniform. Around the world, we study and practice the very same principles of the D.A. Program—that is unity!

We all have heard the phrase "You can only keep what you have by giving it away." In this respect, we need always be aware that our recovery depends on D.A. members carrying the message to the still-suffering debtor. This is our Fifth Tradition, our primary purpose. A newcomer can become confused if our meetings use literature that has not been approved through our World Service Conference's Literature Approval Process, as outlined below.

Conference-approved literature assures that the recovery message therein will be clear and consistent and will reflect the principles of the Twelve Steps and Twelve Traditions of Debtors Anonymous. If a newcomer leaves a meeting confused about the D.A. message because a piece of non-Conference-approved literature was being used, then we have failed in our primary purpose. Outside literature has a place in the recovery process but can conflict with the D.A. message and confuse the newcomer. Our experience has shown that, in the first days of recovery, a newcomer needs firm and solid grounding in the D.A. Program

Tradition Six suggests another important reason why we do not use non-Conference-approved literature for recovery purposes at our meetings. Endorsing the use of any piece of outside literature affiliates D.A. with an outside enterprise, thereby diverting us from our primary purpose. Bookstores abound with shelves of self-help books. A D.A. meeting that uses any of these books is putting the program of Debtors Anonymous at risk of legal action from the authors or publishers of those works. Tradition Four reminds us that each group is autonomous except in matters affecting D.A. as a whole. In this case, using non-Conference-approved material as part of the meeting's format can place the entire Fellowship in jeopardy.

The GSB is not in the business of policing meetings or of telling members what they may or may not read outside our meetings; we are here to safeguard the Traditions and maintain the integrity of the D.A. Program as a whole. However, it is the opinion of the entire General Service Board that any D.A. meeting that insists upon using outside literature as part of its format is in fact not reflecting the principles of unity, and is putting the entire Fellowship at risk.

Meetings that insist upon using non-Conference-approved literature as part of their meeting format are breaking with the Traditions. We would hope that these meetings regard this issue as seriously as we do and, in the interest of unity, reconsider their meeting format.

Suggestions for new literature can come from any D.A. member or group. There is a process for creating and approving new D.A. literature. All pieces go through this process, which involves many committees before it reaches approval by the delegates at the Conference. If you believe there is a need for literature on a certain D.A. topic, we invite you to get involved by sending your idea to the Literature Committee of the World Service Conference or becoming a General Service Representative and attending the Literature Committee of the World Service Conference in person.

B. The Literature Development Process in D.A.

The process by which D.A. develops Conference-approved literature is long and deliberate. When D.A. decides to put its name and trademark or logo on a piece of recovery literature and distributes it as representing the considered conscience of the D.A. Fellowship as a whole and extreme care must be taken. Not only does our literature help to present our public face to the outside world, but also it serves to provide guidance and assistance to the newcomer and still-suffering debtors who have not yet joined our Fellowship.

As the following chart indicates, there must be review by three separate committees, the General Service Board as a whole, and the World Service Conference of Debtors Anonymous. This process ensures that nothing is published without careful thought and the focused insights of many D.A. members. The three committees are:

    a. WSC Literature Committee, which approves the initial concept for a piece of literature and reviews the work in process and before approval by the WSC

    b. Literature Services Committee, which develops the piece by selecting a writer and editing various drafts.

    c. GSB Literature Publishing Committee, which engages in a general supervisory role of the whole process and recommends to the GSB whether a particular draft should be finally accepted and submitted to the WSC Literature Committee for approval.

Anyone in D.A. may suggest the creation of a piece of literature and submit the idea to the GSB or a GSR/ISR. In some cases, a committee of the WSC will develop the concept for a piece of literature relevant to its area of concentration and request the WSC Literature Committee to submit that concept for approval by the WSC. In other cases, the GSB may request the Literature Committee to consider a particular concept. But most frequently, the idea will originate with a GSR or ISR attending the Conference. A GSR/ISR whose group or Intergroup has expressed a desire for a new piece of literature should become a member of the WSC Literature Committee and submit her/his proposal for discussion there. If the Committee agrees that this is a good idea, it can then bring a motion for Conference approval for the writing process to begin.

In addition to Conference-approved literature directed to recovery and unity, the General Service Board also produces service-related literature. Because this literature is intended for use only within D.A., and not for use by newcomers or outsiders, there is less need for recourse to the Conference approval process. Service literature represents an effort to share the experience, strength, and hope of individuals and groups on their journey in carrying their message of recovery to the still-suffering debtor. The General Service Office and the General Service Board can serve as a clearinghouse for this type of information, helping D.A. members to avoid the mistakes of the past and discover new ways of carrying the message. Service literature carries the statement:

This is D.A. service material, produced in response to the needs of D.A. members for information and shared experience on specific service-related subjects. It reflects the guidance of the Twelve Traditions, the General Service Board (GSB), and the General Service Office (GSO), and is developed from the shared experience of D.A. members throughout the Fellowship. Since service material reflects the current and ever-developing conscience of our Fellowship as a whole, it does not undergo the usual D.A. literature approval process, which requires final approval by the World Service Conference (WSC). Instead, service material may be updated periodically under the auspices of the General Service Board to reflect current Fellowship experience.

Service literature represents a rare exception to the idea that only Conference-approved literature may be used at D.A. meetings.

Major Service works such as the Trustee Manual, the Debtors Anonymous Manual for Service,

World Service Conference Host Committee Manual, etc. often 'reside' with a specific trustee committee, which as part of that committee's scope, encompasses the periodic/frequent maintenance of that service material. For example, the Trustee Manual is maintained by the GSB Nominations Committee, the DAMS is maintained by the GSB Long-Range Planning Committee, and the WSC Host Manual is maintained by the GSB Conference Support Committee with input from the WSC Conference Committee.

What is the process for production and approval of Service Material?

1. A GSB committee, or WSC committee via its GSB liaison, submits a concept to the GSB for approval. If approved, that committee determines who will write the material.
2. Final draft of manuscript is submitted to the appropriate GSB Committee for review.
3. If literature is to be on website as a download, the appropriate GSB Committee reviews document and either approves or send suggested revisions to writer.
4. If literature is to be published, the manuscript is submitted to Literature Publications for review. If the trustee committee decides to oversee this part of the process, they will notify Lit Pub of their decision. Lit Pub will then:
   a. Return the manuscript to committee with suggested revisions, or
   b. Send the manuscript to Literature Services (LS) for final editing, or
   c. Approve the manuscript and ask GSB for its approval.
5. Literature Services handles final edited manuscript, submitting manuscript and costs to Literature Publications for its final approval.
6. Lit Publications sends final manuscript to the appropriate GSB committee to submit to the GSB for its final approval.

Service Material Approval Process approved by D.A. GSB April 2013

The Debtors Anonymous Literature Approval Process

(Revision of Process approved in 2008, approved by 2013 WSC)

Stage 1: Approval of concept and writer

1.	At the World Service Conference, the WSC Literature Committee proposes a concept for new or revised literature, along with suggested mediums, and makes a motion for approval of that concept at Convocation. Should the Board or the WSC Literature Committee vote by substantial unanimity to alter or rescind the concept, the WSC must be informed of the action and the reasoning for their decision.
2.	If the motion passes, the WSC Literature Committee creates a detailed outline or similar guide for the writer and forwards to the General Service Board's (GSB) Literature Publications Committee. If BDA literature, the outline is created by the WSC BDA committee and forwarded to WSC Literature Committee for approval. Literature Publications reviews the outline and determines if the concept requires a volunteer or paid writer. Literature Services creates a Request for Proposals (RFP), which is distributed to the Fellowship. *For volunteer writers* Literature Services and Literature Publications jointly review candidates' samples and choose a writer. The GSB Legal Affairs Committee estimates the monetary value of the piece (in-kind donation) and issues a contract to the writer. *For paid writers* Literature Services reviews candidates' samples and bids, selects a writer, and requests GSB Literature Publications Committee to approve the writer. If the writer is approved, GSB Literature Publications makes a motion to the full GSB to approve the selected writer. If the writer is approved by the GSB, GSB Legal Affairs creates a contract, to be approved by Literature Publications and Finance Committee.
3.	The WSC Literature Committee's Board Liaison informs the committee of approved and contracted writer.
4.	Writer submits first new sample (amount of material determined by Literature Services) to Literature Services for its review. Literature Services reviews and either invites writer to revise or submits to GSB Literature Publications for review. Literature Services and GSB Literature Publications meet jointly to determine if project should continue with that writer.

Stage 2: Development of manuscript

1.	Literature Services asks writer to either continue writing or revise sample as per Literature Services and GSB Literature Publications comments. For longer projects, the writer should submit sections for approval, rather than a complete manuscript.
2.	Writer submits complete manuscript, or agreed upon sections, to Literature Services. Literature Services determines whether further revisions are required.
3.	Once Literature Services has approved a revised manuscript (or section of longer manuscript, as appropriate), it is submitted to GSB Literature Publications for general approval of format and organization and additional comments. If Lit Pub approve, Literature Services submits manuscript with comments to WSC Literature Committee for general approval of format and organization and additional comments. If BDA literature, it is also sent to the WSC BDA committee.
	If Lit Pub does not approve, Literature Services and GSB Literature Publications meet jointly to discuss next steps.
4.	Literature Services receives and reviews WSC Literature Committee and/or BDA comments and requests revisions from the writer. Literature Services determines whether even further revisions are required.

Stage 3: Final Approval

1.	Writer submits final draft to Literature Services for final edits.
2.	Edited final draft goes to GSB Literature Publications for review and approval. If approved, the edited final draft goes to GSB for approval. If not approved, Literature Services and GSB Literature Publications meet jointly to discuss next steps.
3.	If final edited draft is approved by the GSB, it is returned to the WSC Literature Committee for approval. If approved, only minor editorial comments will be considered at this point. The current WSC Literature Committee makes a recommendation to the incoming WSC Literature Committee. If BDA Literature, it is also sent to WSC BDA committee.
4.	Incoming WSC Literature Committee receives final draft at the next WSC and brings a motion at Convocation to approve publication of the piece of literature. Only minor editorial changes will be considered at WSC before publication.

C. Use of A.A. Literature

We study the literature of Alcoholics Anonymous® to strengthen our understanding of compulsive disease.

– Eighth Tool of Debtors Anonymous

Why Do We Read A.A. Literature?

Alcoholics Anonymous® (A.A.) was the first 12-Step program and has been very successful in helping alcoholics recover from their disease. Debtors Anonymous (D.A.) has yet to develop its own literature to the extent A.A. has. So, we read A.A. literature to better understand our own compulsive behavior. A.A. literature shows us how A.A. members have used the 12 Steps for their individual recovery and the 12 Traditions to develop and protect their Fellowship. We find that these 12 Traditions are just as crucial to maintaining the D.A. Fellowship.

How Do We Use A.A. Literature?

Without D.A. most of us have found that we are powerless to stop incurring unsecured debt. Many of us were surprised to learn that incurring unsecured debt is a compulsion. By substituting in our minds "incurring unsecured debt" for "drinking" and "compulsive debtor" for "alcoholic" in the A.A. literature, we can identify the compulsive, self-destructive patterns described. In the past, many of us may not have seen the connection between ourselves and alcoholics. However, upon surrendering to our powerlessness over unsecured debt, we find we can identify closely with the compulsive behavior of the alcoholic.

In reading A.A. literature, we can see how our compulsive behavior resembles the alcoholic's drinking behavior. The following are examples of our common experiences:

- Breaking promises not to drink/incur unsecured debt again.

- Trying to fix the symptom rather than the underlying problem, e.g., "consolidating" debt leads to more debt just as "switching drinks" provides the illusion of a cure to the alcoholic.

- Incurring unsecured debt and feeling elated as an alcoholic does when drinking; the later feeling hopeless to find a way out afterward.

- Using credit to feel grown-up and like we are "enough."

- Like the alcoholic who continues to drink, believing that "this time it will be different," we continue to incur unsecured debt, believing this time it will work out okay for the better.

- Believing we can handle our problems ourselves.

These are just a handful of the many examples of compulsive behavior illustrated in A.A. literature. We suggest you read the A.A. literature to find similarities that fit your individual situation.

What Types of A.A. Literature Do We Use?

D.A. members find they benefit greatly from most of the A.A. literature available. The main sources of information are Alcoholics Anonymous®, commonly known as the Big Book® and The Twelve Steps and Twelve Traditions.

The Big Book® talks at length about the compulsion and tells many stories of A.A. members and their experiences of recovery. It explains the basic concepts of the Twelve Step program and the spiritual changes necessary to be relieved of our compulsion to incur unsecured debt. The Twelve Steps and Twelve Traditions takes us through the Twelve Steps of recovery more in detail.

Some specific D.A. issues are addressed in the A.A. literature. For example, on page 79 of the Big Book®, we read of a man who owed alimony and thus was in debt to his ex-wife. We read how he wrote a letter to her suggesting what and how he could pay and how he started making payments as a Ninth Step amend.

We also read about work and money issues on pages 120-122 of The Twelve Steps and Twelve Traditions. We see that some of the first alcoholics recovering in A.A. had money problems as well as the compulsion of alcoholic drinking. The Twelve Step spiritual recovery program had to be applied to all areas of their lives, not just alcohol. In the same way, we realize we can apply the Twelve Steps to all areas of our lives, not just those involving unsecured debt.

As described on page 82 of the Big Book®, a person who has only stopped drinking is like

> ...the farmer who came up out of his cyclone cellar to find his home ruined. To his wife, he remarked, "Don't see anything the matter here, Ma. Ain't it grand the wind stopped blowing?"

This story reminds us that not incurring unsecured debt is just the beginning. We see that we must have a spiritual change if we want to be relieved of our desire to incur unsecured debt.

D.A. members can also benefit from other A.A. literature such as A.A. Comes of Age, Pass It On, and Doctor Bob and the Good Oldtimers, which relate the history of A.A. We have found that reading about the history of A.A. and its Twelve Traditions can help us in our own D.A. Program.

What Other Types of Literature Do We Use in D.A.?

D.A. does not endorse any literature outside of its own General Service Conference—approved literature. A better understanding of why D.A. doesn't endorse any other literature can be found by reading the chapter on A.A.'s Tradition Six ("An A.A. group ought never endorse, finance, or lend the A.A. name to any related facility or outside enterprise, lest problems of money, property, and prestige divert us from our primary purpose.") in The Twelve Steps and Twelve Traditions. However, our program encourages the use of outside sources.

Where Can You Get A.A. Literature?

You can purchase A.A. literature at some D.A. meetings. Literature may also be obtained from local open meetings of A.A. Each meeting may differ in what literature it carries. If it is not available there, A.A. has local area Intergroups all over the country and in many places abroad. Check your local directory for their phone number.

D. Copyrights, Trademarks, and Other Intellectual Property

In our service activities, we must never forget the importance of protecting D.A.'s intellectual property rights to prevent the loss of trademarks or copyrights on our publications, name, and service mark. History and law books are full of examples of authors and publishers who have lost control over their publications and trade names or trademarks because of improper use or failure to police. We hope never to see a credit card or finance company using our name, trademark, or literature to promote their ends. Yet, this can happen if we fail to be vigilant in protecting our intellectual property rights.

In the haste of preparing a flyer or setting up a meeting or workshop, it is easy to forget that D.A. has a registered trademark on the following symbol:

This symbol should be used with care and only when it is clear that all possible issues related to the Twelve Traditions of D.A. have been settled. The D.A. General Service Board has granted expressly limited permission to registered D.A. groups and Intergroups to use this symbol for communications within their memberships in furtherance of only D.A. service purposes. This permission is only for the purposes specified or enumerated here, and explicitly does not extend to any other use or activity unless approved by the General Service Board in writing.

However, if there is to be any distribution of the material outside the immediate group or Intergroup, specific written permission should be obtained from the General Service Board to use it.

Similar care must be exercised in utilizing D.A. literature. Again, the General Service Board has granted expressly limited permission to D.A. groups and Intergroups to reprint short excerpts from D.A. copyrighted material in furtherance of the goals of Twelve Step service. However, any such use should be accompanied by a notation of D.A.'s copyright and an indication that the material is reproduced by permission of the D.A. General Service Board. The following notice is sufficient:

© Debtors Anonymous General Service Board, Inc. Reproduced with permission.

Again, care must be taken not to use extensive amounts of material. It is a violation of D.A.'s copyright to reproduce entire pamphlets or parts of pamphlets or other publications without written express permission from the D.A. General Service Board. Care must also be taken to ensure that quoted material is used in an appropriate context and with awareness of the Twelve Traditions of D.A. In general, if more than a few sentences from D.A. literature are to be reproduced for any reason, it is requested that the D.A. member, group or Intergroup quoting from the D.A. literature consult with the General Service Board prior to said use.

Special care must be taken regarding the use of D.A.'s intellectual property on the Internet. A D.A. group, Intergroup, or individual member runs the risk of diluting the D.A. rights to its name and symbol by using them on the Internet without written express permission. Because of the widespread accessibility of the Internet to outsiders and those who might easily be confused by mistakes, errors, or violations of the Twelve Traditions, the D.A. General Service Board has not granted permission to use the D.A. name or symbol or D.A. literature on the Internet. Any such use requires the written express permission of the General Service Board. This requirement applies to the creation of websites using the D.A. name or symbol or reproducing D.A. literature in whole or in part.

E. Respect for trademarks and copyrights of other fellowships

As responsible members of D.A., we do not borrow or use copyrighted materials from other twelve-step fellowships.

Below, we offer some guidance from Alcoholics Anonymous World Services, Inc. as an example:

A.A. World Services and the Grapevine have registered a number of trademarks and logos, and the guidelines for using them are based partly on legal considerations and partly on the nature of A.A. The following is a complete list of registered trademarks and service marks that symbolize Alcoholics Anonymous, its work and its purpose: A.A.; Alcoholics Anonymous; The Big Book; Box 4-5-9; The Grapevine; A.A. Grapevine; GV; Box 1980, La Viña.

Use of these marks on goods or services that do not emanate from A.A., and have not been approved by A.A., both infringes upon and dilutes A.A. marks, in legal terms. The resulting harm is that the marks and A.A. itself, since A.A. is what the marks symbolize, will come to be associated with a variety of products and services that are not part of A.A., and are not consistent with A.A.'s purpose. This will cause the marks to lose their meaning and significance as symbols of Alcoholics Anonymous. [5]

---

5   Intellectual Property Policies approved by the AAWS Board, January 27, 2005 and revised March 2011. https://aa.org/pages/en_US/intellectual-property-policies cited on July 18, 2021.

CHAPTER 9 – THE GENERAL SERVICE BOARD

A. Frequently Asked Questions about Becoming a D.A. General Service Board Trustee

Adopted by the GSB 1995 [6]

What is the Debtors Anonymous General Service Board?

The Debtors Anonymous General Service Board, Inc. (D.A. GSB) is a 501(c)(3) not-for-profit organization incorporated in the State of New York. The General Service Board is the chief service arm of the D.A. World Service Conference and is essentially custodial in its character.

Who are the General Service Board Trustees?

The GSB bylaws establish a minimum of three (3) and a maximum of fifteen (15) Trustees, including a maximum of ten (10) Class A compulsive debtor Trustees and a maximum of five (5) non-debtor Trustees. Class A Trustees are those who have arrested their compulsive debting, have not incurred new, unsecured debt for a period of at least three years and who are living so far as possible within the principles of the Debtors Anonymous Twelve Steps. Class B Trustees are those who are not now and have not been afflicted by the disease of compulsive debting and who express a profound faith in the D.A. program. Trustees elect their own successors from among all interested parties, subject to ratification at the next annual Conference.

What is the purpose of the General Service Board?

The following excerpt from the bylaws of the General Service Board describes the primary function of the General Service Board as a whole:

> *"The Corporation (Debtors Anonymous General Service Board, Inc.) shall use its best efforts to ensure that the Traditions are maintained, for the Corporation is regarded by the Fellowship as the custodian of the Traditions and, accordingly, the Corporation shall not itself nor, so far as it is within its power to do so, permit others to modify, alter, or amplify the Traditions, except in keeping with the provisions of the Certificate of Incorporation (the 'Certificate') and the bylaws of the Corporation (the 'bylaws'). The Corporation shall put forth its best efforts within the context of the Conference, Articles of Incorporation, and these bylaws to protect the Twelve Traditions."*

What else does the GSB do?

The Trustees are responsible for managing the day-to-day affairs of the D.A. program, including maintaining D.A.'s financial records, managing D.A.'s cash flow, overseeing the D.A. General Service Office and employees, maintaining the D.A. Web site and other communications channels, reviewing and publishing D.A. literature, taking ultimate responsibility for the annual World Service Conference, and responding to requests from D.A. members, newcomers, professionals, journalists, and other members of the public.

How do the Trustees work together?

GSB Trustees meet twice a year in person—in late summer they meet for two days prior to the start the annual D.A. World Service Conference, and in the late winter/early spring they meet for a long weekend. During the rest of the year, the Board meets on two-hour conference calls, spaced approximately six weeks apart. In addition, each Trustee serves on several Board committees and participates in the work of those committees via email and conference calls. Each trustee also serves as a liaison to a World Service Conference committee and/or caucus.

---

6   Revised 2007, 2009, 2010, 2012.

How long do GSB Trustees serve?

GSB Trustees serve for a three-year term, and may renew their service for another three-year term, for a total of six consecutive years. New Trustees may be elected at any time during the year and begin their term at the WSC. If there is a vacancy on the Board they may join immediately, however, their term of office begins when they are ratified at a World Service Conference. It is suggested that upon completion of their board service, Trustees will refrain from serving as part of the World Service structure again, including the positions of Trustee, Appointed Committee Member (ACM), General Service Representative (GSR), or Intergroup Service Representative (ISR). However, former Trustees may be invited to serve in a non-voting capacity as special workers or Project Contributors.

What are the suggested qualifications to become a Class A Trustee?

The General Service Board of Debtors Anonymous has found that the following attributes are those that contribute most towards being able to fulfill a General Service Board commitment. It is suggested that a GSB Class A Trustee nominee would:

1. Be a member of D.A. who regularly attends meetings, has a sponsor and is a sponsor, has and sits on pressure relief groups, and has at least three years of not incurring any new unsecured debt.
2. Be committed to working the Twelve Steps of D.A.
3. Have a desire to seek the will of a Higher Power, however one may conceive of a Higher Power.
4. Be committed to service as a principle of life; have a willingness and desire to grow through service with the knowledge that it will have its challenges, requires a definite commitment of time, and that world service takes priority over other service.
5. Be dedicated to and active in D.A. service, as demonstrated by successful completion of service commitments on an ongoing basis, including experience and participation as a GSR or ISR in at least one World Service Conference.
6. Have the ability to follow through with commitments and show willingness to complete those commitments in accordance with D.A. principles, D.A. Tools, the Twelve Steps and the Twelve Traditions.
7. Have a desire and the ability to perform leadership roles in the spirit of being a trusted servant rather than a ruler and have the ability to work independently while at the same time being part of a team.
8. Be dedicated and committed to the health of D.A. and have a desire to carry the message to the still suffering debtor.
9. Understand the difference between majority rule and group conscience and be willing to work within the group conscience.
10. Have a flexible attitude and the ability to work with other people, even if the direction was not the first choice.
11. Have reliable and private access to a telephone, a computer, a printer, and email.
12. Have effective communication skills, including the ability to listen to others and speak honestly, the ability to write and deliver reports, the ability to follow-up on messages and engage in the group process with the GSB, and to the ability to use the telephone, email, and the Internet.
13. Have good time management and organizational skills.
14. Have the ability to travel twice a year or more on GSB business.
15. Have the willingness to use one's full name, address, telephone number, and email address in order to communicate effectively with the GSB and the General Service Office, and to carry out various GSB duties, such as negotiating contracts.

What are the suggested qualifications to become a Class B Trustee?

1. The GSB seeks Class B trustee candidates with significant 12-Step Fellowship service experience and professional skills in finance, law, and nonprofit administration.
2. Prior nonprofit board experience is a plus.
3. Have reliable and private access to a telephone, a computer, a printer, and email.
4. Have the ability to travel twice a year or more on GSB business.

What are the legal responsibilities of trustees of not-for-profit boards?

Under well-established principles of nonprofit corporation law, a board member must meet certain standards of conduct and attention in carrying out their responsibilities to the organization. These standards are usually described as the Duty of Care, the Duty of Loyalty and the Duty of Obedience.

1. **Duty of Care:** The duty of care describes the level of competence that is expected of a board member, and is commonly expressed as the duty of "care that an ordinarily prudent person would exercise in a like position and under similar circumstances." This means that a board member owes the duty to exercise reasonable care when he or she makes a decision as a steward of the organization.
2. **Duty of Loyalty:** The duty of loyalty is a standard of faithfulness; a board member must give undivided allegiance when making decisions affecting the organization. This means that a board member can never use information obtained as a member for personal gain, but must act in the best interests of the organization.
3. **Duty of Obedience:** The duty of obedience requires board members to be faithful to the organization's mission. They are not permitted to act in a way that is inconsistent with the central goals of the organization. A basis for this rule lies in the public's trust that the organization will manage donated funds to fulfill the organization's mission.

How do I nominate myself for GSB Trustee?

GSB nominees should fill out the online form at https://debtorsanonymous.org/gsbapply and submit a nomination package consisting of:

1. **A Letter of Intent:** This is a letter from the nominee stating their interest in GSB Service and that he or she meets the guidelines as described for a Class A or Class B Trustee. Please be sure to include all contact information, including full name, address, telephone number, and email address.
2. **A Service Resume:** A resume/biography of the nominee showing prior D.A. service, other Twelve Step service, and any qualifications or experience that may be helpful to the D.A. General Service Board.
3. **A Letter of Recommendation:** A signed letter from the nominating person or group making the nomination and stating their knowledge of the nominee's experience in a service role or activity.
4. (Optional) A professional resume may also be useful in evaluating the professional skills a candidate could bring to the Board.

Where do I send the nomination package?

The three items (or four, if including the optional professional resume) in the nomination package should ideally be emailed as an attachment (in Word, rtf, pdf, or jpeg formats) to the GSB Nominations Committee, c/o the General Service Office at office@debtorsanonymous.org. The package can also be mailed to the GSB Nominations Committee c/o the General Service Office, PO Box 920888, Needham, MA 02492-0009; however, keep in mind that email capability is essential to being able to serve effectively on the General Service Board.

Who can nominate a candidate?

Any interested party, including but not limited to, any past or present GSB Trustee, any D.A. member, D.A. group, D.A. Intergroup, or collection thereof, may nominate a candidate. All members of D.A. and friends of D.A. are encouraged to suggest possible candidates to serve as Class B Trustees by emailing nominations@debtorsanonymous.org

What is the deadline for submitting a nomination?

New Trustees begin their service when they are ratified at the annual World Service Conference. Nominations should be received by the Nominations Committee by April 1. If approved, the new Trustee will begin serving at the next World Service Conference. If there is an opening, they can begin serving immediately

How will I be notified if my nomination has been approved?

The chair of the Nominations Committee will notify each nominee of the outcome of the GSB review process by email.

What happens if my nomination is not approved?

The GSB reviews each candidate's qualifications carefully. The review process includes interviewing each candidate by telephone. The GSB is looking for candidates who have a history of consistent and effective D.A. service, a willingness to serve D.A. as a whole, and the ability to work well in the context of the spiritual group conscience process. Sometimes, after reviewing a candidate's service history, the GSB declines to approve a nomination. This does not mean that the candidate may not apply again in the future, after gaining more experience in D.A. recovery and service.

Why should I consider becoming a D.A. Trustee?

1. To give back what I've been given.
2. To help D.A. live, prosper, and grow.
3. To maintain my own recovery.
4. To demonstrate the power of service to transform lives.
5. To understand how our organization operates.
6. To learn how to apply the D.A. Steps, Traditions, and Concepts to our service work.
7. To gain humility.
8. To practice leadership skills in a spiritual context.
9. To work with trusted servants who are working a rigorous recovery program.

B. How the General Service Board Functions

GSB Mission Statement

As Trustees of Debtors Anonymous, we are stewards and trusted servants attempting to follow the spiritual principles expressed through the group conscience of the Fellowship of Debtors Anonymous. As custodians of the 12 Steps and 12 Traditions, we practice those spiritual principles in all our endeavors.

Outline of GSB Trustee service commitment

The General Service Board of Debtors Anonymous is made up of debtors and non-debtors who desire to serve the D.A. Fellowship in the capacity of world service. Having demonstrated ability and enthusiasm for D.A. service, they are carefully recommended to the GSB by their peers. After being elected by the existing GSB and ratified by the D.A. Convocation, these individuals are called upon by the fellowship to be the "Trustees," those entrusted by the World Service Conference and the Fellowship at large with the ongoing stewardship of D.A., the 12 Steps, the 12 Traditions, and the 12 Concepts for World Service.

Service to the General Service Board of Trustees (GSB) and its Committees

The General Service Board of Trustees, Inc. is responsible for putting into practice D.A.'s group conscience as expressed through the will of the World Service Conference (WSC). The Board also fulfills all fiduciary responsibilities required of nonprofit corporations by law; the Trustees have serious legal duties that they perform, such as protecting copyrights and service marks and filing required forms and tax returns. The D.A. General Service Office (GSO) assists the GSB and its committees in carrying out these responsibilities. In addition to fulfilling its fiduciary and legal functions, the GSB also serves as D.A.'s primary administrative leadership. [7]

Structure of the GSB

The GSB may consist of up to fifteen (15) Trustees—a maximum of ten (10) recovering debtors and a maximum of five (5) non-debtors. The GSB elects its own officers: Chair, Vice-Chair, Treasurer, Assistant Treasurer, and Secretary. A number of GSB committees both carry out the wishes of the World Conference and develop new projects to benefit the Fellowship. Committees are created and dissolved as necessary by the GSB. Some of the committees are: Executive, Communications and Technology, Conference Support, Finance, Audit and Legal Affairs, Literature/Publications, Long-Range Planning, Office, Nominations and Procedures, Public Information, and Literature Translations and Licensing.

A Trustee also serves as a Liaison to one or more of the World Conference Committees: Conference, Internal Operations, Resource Development, Fellowship Communications, International, Public Information, Business Debtors Anonymous, Technology, Literature and Underserved and Under-represented Outreach. Trustees also act as liaisons to two informal caucuses: Intergroup and Spiritually sustainable Earning.

In view of these responsibilities, there is a certain level of commitment expected from GSB Trustees. It is expected that Trustees participate in GSB conference calls and committee conference calls in a timely manner. If a Trustee is unable to participate in a call, the Chair of the GSB or committee should be notified in advance. It is the responsibility of each Trustee to have their work represented on the conference call.

It is expected that as Trustees, board members have the desire and the time available to be good to their word. Committees, subcommittees, and projects that Trustees make commitments to need to be completed in a timely manner. When a work item cannot be completed, the Trustee should let the committee chair know in advance.

How Work Gets Done on the General Service Board

The D.A. GSB meets as a group twice a year face-to-face, in the days prior to the World Service Conference, and also in the late winter or early spring. Between these face-to-face meetings, we meet by conference call. We use a conference call service, dial a special telephone number at a designated time. Our phone calls are generally two hours long. On rare occasions, we may set a special call to deal with a specific pressing issue. A lot of work is also done between calls via email.

GSB Committees

In preparation for the GSB conference calls, each GSB committee meets by telephone to discuss issues relating to the scope of the committee. Committees set their own call schedules. Committees elect their own officers. Committee secretaries take minutes and email the minutes to the entire GSB after the call. The GSB chair compiles each committee's minutes into the next GSB call packet. Note: If a committee secretary forgets to email minutes to the chair, then there will be

---

7   See Concept Eight for further amplification.

no written record of the committee's work in the next call packet.

Bringing Motions

Motions during the GSB phone call can come from committees or from an individual Trustee. Non-GSB members do not have the standing to make motions or attend GSB calls. If a committee or caucus of the World Service Conference wants to undertake an action that needs GSB approval, the GSB liaison brings a motion to the GSB call on their behalf.

Actions that need full GSB approval include activities that involve the expenditure of money, with the exception of Office-related expenses up to $100; approval of all literature, including Board-produced essays; anything that could be construed as controversial within or outside the organization; in general, communications to WSC committees, caucuses, groups, Intergroups, and members; and any activity affecting D.A. as a whole, such as statements on D.A. policy or outreach from the GSB to the public. All matters should be referred to the full Board for discussion and decision; this ensures that decisions will be reflected in the Board minutes.

Actions that do not need full Board approval include how GSB committees choose to operate internally, such as policies, rules, and procedures that the committee adopts for itself; and actions that normally fall within its usual scope and purview—for example, approving the reprinting of literature is a normal activity of the Finance Committee with input from Literature Publications. Requests for information sent to outside entities such as vendors or experts do not generally need to come before the Board, unless the request may have some larger consequences. When in doubt, bring the issue as a motion to the full Board for discussion, either through a committee or as an individual.

Motions requesting funding should be presented with a proposal and a spending plan that has been reviewed by Finance. Whenever possible, motions should have clear action plans with timelines and responsible parties.

All GSB decisions requiring action should be noted in the secretary's Minutes along with deadlines and responsible parties.

Committee Work

Much of the work of each GSB committee is focused on addressing the list of issues and concerns that were assigned to it at the Conference. At the end of the year, the committee is expected to report on the disposition of each issue to the Fellowship. The committee is also encouraged to think proactively, creatively, and long-term about what it can do to help D.A.

How the GSB Communicates to the Fellowship

The GSB has several means to communicate to the Fellowship.

- The *DA Focus*, our quarterly service newsletter, is available on the D.A. website and emailed to anyone who subscribes to eNews. The GSB also utilizes eNews announcements to send out flyers publicizing new literature, as well as flyers and forms from the WSC Committees and Caucuses. Occasionally, the GSB mails letters to the Fellowship.

- The GSB has on three occasions written and produced essays on issues that seemed crucial to D.A. as a whole. (Group inventory, use of Conference-approved literature, and how to keep a meeting alive.) These were considered service literature and therefore were allowed to bypass the literature approval process. These essays are available for free on the website.

- Sometimes D.A. Trustees write articles for the *Ways & Means*, but that publication is considered D.A.'s meeting in print, and it is understood that the Trustee is speaking as a D.A. member, not as a representative of the GSB.

- The D.A. website is also a means of communication.

- Finally, Trustees communicate formally and informally to and through D.A. members they meet, including delegates who attend the World Service Conference, members of the Host Committee, and D.A. people they meet wherever they travel to hold their Face to Face (F2F) meetings.

Editorial Policy

The *DA Focus* and the D.A. website are service-related communication vehicles, and as such, do not publish or post any recovery-related material that is not already Conference-approved.

D.A. Publications Advisory Statement (GSB 2005)

> *Since all publications cannot go through the conference approval process, the D.A. World Service Conference recognizes that the Ways & Means is by tradition the international meeting in print of D.A. The Steps, Traditions and Concepts are our guidelines, always wishing to reflect D.A. and nothing but D.A. The DA Focus and the D.A. Web site are service publications for the D.A. Fellowship.*
>
> *—Presented at the 2005 WSC by the General Service Board.*

In 2008, the World Service Conference also approved the concept of posting D.A. recovery stories on the D.A. website.

Working with the GSO

Any Trustee can ask the Office Manager questions; however, before asking them to do something for us, we need to be mindful of the workload. Always remember to copy the Office liaison on your request, so there is a sense of the workload that is coming from Trustees, to help the Office Manager manage their time.

Privacy and Anonymity

By custom, we don't generally give out each other's email addresses to members of the Fellowship without getting permission. We also refrain from publishing our full names in any document or communication that might be posted on the Internet. We are cautious with confidential Board materials in our homes and when we are at the WSC, Face to Face, or any other location where anonymity may accidentally be broken.

The Role of the Board Liaison (to each WSC Committee)

- Is a link or conduit between the Board and the committee.

- Promotes and advocates the use of the 12 Concepts and 12 Traditions.

- Gets the committee's questions to the Board answered.

- Acts as the contact to the GSB for the committee and for the committee to the GSB.

- Is a trusted servant to the committee.

- May act as an historical reference/resource.

- During the year, acts as the interface with the committee chair.

- Reports to the GSB regarding committee activities.

- Reports to the committee relevant GSB actions.

- Attends committee sessions, whenever possible, but does not vote.

How to Resolve a Conflict between a WSC Committee and a GSB Liaison:

1. The committee chair contacts the GSB chair. If a conflict with the GSB chair, the WSC committee chair would contact the Executive Committee of the GSB, with the chair not participating.
2. The GSB chair (or Executive Committee) reviews situation with the committee chair.
3. The GSB chair (or Executive Committee) reviews the situation with the Liaison.
4. Together, they seek a spiritual solution based on the 12 Traditions and 12 Concepts.

C. Spiritual problem solving

a. Some of the goals of Spiritual Problem Solving

- Circumvent repetitive negative patterns

- Use a humanistic approach when working with others

- Develop and nurture respect and compassion for each other

- No shame or blame

- Reduce our frustration level

- Bring our personal and organizational recovery to a new level

- Further the work of D.A. as a whole

b. Spiritual Problem Solving: SPS
1. Identify and define the specific nature of the conflict.
2. Generate as many solutions as possible in a brainstorming fashion.
3. Evaluate the strengths and weaknesses of each solution.
4. Prioritize the solutions in the order they are most likely to succeed.
5. Begin work on the solution most likely to succeed with the support and encouragement of the rest of the committee.
6. If the first solution does not work, the members try the second-best solution, and so forth. Usually, the first one works well.

c. The Spiritual Part
1. Acknowledge the individual(s) and the contribution they have made so far.
2. Listen for a deeper understanding of the person and their issue (it is not necessary to get involved in the details of personal issues unless you want to).
3. Gently suggest that the individual(s) seek help from appropriate sources (go to meetings, call your sponsor, schedule a PRG).
4. Leave room for the individual(s) to be part of the solution, if they so choose.
5. Maintain an attitude of compassion; principles, not personalities; no shame, or blame. We are in this together, supporting each other, seeking recovery.

Note:
1. Every plan or project needs a specific, reasonable timeline.
2. While it sometimes seems that one person is causing a roadblock, we usually all play a role in every interaction. It helps if everyone involved takes their own private inventory no matter what the circumstances.

Suggestions for group decision making
1. Write down the problem or issue you feel is most important.
2. Record all problems and issues on a master list.

3. Generate and distribute the list to each member with the problems or issues numbered in no particular order.
4. Request that each member rank-order the top five problems or issues by assigning five points to their most important perceived problem and one point to the least important problem.
5. Tally the results by adding the points for each problem or issue.
6. The problem or issue with the highest number is the most important one for the team based on the collective group conscience.
7. Discuss the results and generate a final ranked list for action planning.

D. GSB Committees

Audit and Legal Affairs Committee

The Audit Committee and Legal Affairs Committee combined in 2018 to become the Audit and Legal Affairs Committee. The committee engages an independent accounting firm to conduct a review of the General Service Board's annual financial statements and meets with that firm to receive and discuss their report. The committee will confirm and assure the independence of the independent accounting firm. It will discuss any weaknesses in internal controls, whether there were any adjustments not recorded on the books, whether the Corporation is following the most appropriate and best accounting principles and whether or not management conducts itself with the highest level of integrity.

The committee is involved in the registration, maintenance, and defense of D.A.'s intellectual property, copyrights, and trademarks. This includes all D.A. logos, literature, and service material, whether in print or other media. The committee works in cooperation with the Literature Publications Committee of the GSB to address copyrights and infringement, preparation of work-for-hire agreements, and many other contract issues for the GSB.

The committee is not limited by the above criteria and should discuss any issues that may be of a concern to any member.

Communications and Technology Committee (CommTech)

The Communications and Technology Committee of the GSB oversees the creation and online publication of the quarterly recovery magazine, *Ways & Means*®, and the quarterly service newsletter, the *DA Focus*. It approves proposals by WSC Committees and Caucuses to host Fellowship-wide calls, makes the recordings of speaker shares from those events available as free podcasts, and manages the content of the D.A. website. CommTech designs and distributes eNews announcements to the D.A. mailing list (members may sign up at debtorsanonymous.org/eNews).

They are also charged with recommending, implementing, and overseeing the use of technology in conducting the administrative business of D.A., keeping with the 12 Traditions and the 12 Concepts of World Service. CommTech assists in the selection and purchasing of computer equipment and software for the office, implements all database handling procedures, oversees creation and maintenance of the website, handles online communications, and plans for future technology needs.

Conference Support Committee (CSC)

The Conference Support Committee works with the WSC Conference Committee on matters of WSC policy and relations between the GSB and the WSC. The CSC also supports WSC delegates, and acts in an advisory capacity to make recommendations to the GSB regarding the production of the D.A. World Service Conference, including site selection, lodging and meals, and local host committee relations.

Executive Committee

The Executive Committee consists of the officers of the GSB: Chair, Vice-Chair, Secretary, Treasurer, and one other Class B Trustee. The Executive Committee meets only when there is an urgent business matter that cannot wait for the next full Board conference call.

Finance Committee

Chaired by the Treasurer, the Finance Committee handles all of the financial information for the D.A. General Service Board, including but not limited to creating the Spending Plan, overseeing the bookkeeper and accountants, reporting financial information to the Fellowship, making recommendations on revenue, expenses, pricing, and Cost of Goods Sold. De facto members of the committee are the Treasurer, Assistant Treasurer, and GSB Chair.

International Committee

Created in 2012, the International General Service Board Committee is charged with a scope to include outreach to and communication with non-US groups.

Literature Publications Committee (LitPub)

The Literature Publications Committee handles all facets of the literature review and publication process. The Literature Publications oversees the literature creation and approval process that involves the Conference Literature Committee, Literature Services (a Board level subcommittee of LitPub), and independent subcontracting writers. The LitPub committee acts as the facilitator and administrator for all proposed D.A. literature, reviewing it for adherence to the Traditions as well as providing general proofreading. This committee then determines whether or not to recommend the piece for approval to the full GSB, which then either approves the piece or disapproves it. Once approved by the GSB, the literature is sent to the Literature Committee of the World Service Conference and if approved, to the Conference floor for vote. If not approved, the literature piece returns to Literature Services for revision. (See the Literature Creation and Approval Process chart for more information.)

Another purpose of Literature Publications is to carry the message of D.A. through literature and electronic media, including audiotapes, CDs, and video. It facilitates the publication and distribution of all D.A. conference-approved and GSB-approved service literature and media. It also develops policies and procedures for publishing, distributing, and granting permission to use D.A. media. It works with the Conference Literature Committee, the Conference Resource Development Committee, Literature Services, the GSB Public Information Committee, GSB Audit and Legal Affairs Committee (for copyrights), Literature Translations and Licensing (for D.A. copyrighted materials) and the GSB Communications and Technology Committee.

Literature Translations and Licensing Committee (LTL)

The Literature Translations and Licensing Committee was created in 2018 to gather and consolidate D.A.'s translation and licensing activities into one committee rather than having the work spread out over several different committees.

Literature Translations and Licensing has two principal areas of activity: it endeavors to ensure a consistent translation process for D.A. groups and Intergroups around the world, working to translate D.A. literature into different languages, and it oversees the licensing of D.A. copyrighted literature and service material, whether in print or other media.

Long-Range Planning Committee (LRPC)

The Long-Range Planning Committee facilitates the GSB's long-term efforts to carry the message of recovery to suffering compulsive debtors around the world. It develops strategies and action plans to help D.A. remain a prosperous, effective Fellowship so that D.A. can fulfill its primary purpose. It works through the GSB to help all levels of D.A.—the GSB, the GSO, the World Service Conference, and the Fellowship—plan and work to establish a strong foundation for the future of D.A.

Nominations and Procedures Committee (NomPro)

The Nominations Committee is responsible for recruiting, revising, selecting, and recommending nominations for both Class A and Class B Trustees. The Nominations Committee maintains a record of past and current Trustees. The Committee also handles the election of GSB officers by receiving candidates' resumes and distributing the information to the Board at the Spring Face to Face GSB meeting and conducting officer elections at the WSC. The Nominations Committee maintains the GSB Trustee Manual, updating it as necessary, and distributes it to new Trustees. In 2020, the committee added reviewing D.A. procedures as part of their responsibilities.

Office Committee (Office)

The GSB Office Committee, acting in both a managerial and advisory capacity, provides a channel for the concerns of the Office Manager to the full Board for action, sets standards for office operations, makes personnel decisions, provides support to the Office, and, in general, oversees the smooth workings of the GSO.

Public Information Committee (PI)

The Public Information Committee of the GSB works closely with the WSC PI Committee to carry the message of D.A. to the outside world. The GSB PI Committee works with the media through the Media Contact Person (MCP), a position created in 2006; creates tools; forwards requests; and ensures all communications follow the Traditions.

E. Financial Information

Trustee Reimbursement

All Board-related expenses may be reimbursed by submitting a reimbursement form to the GSO.

Trustee Travel Policy: [8]

Travel Planning and Arrangements

Travel arrangements will be coordinated through the current Treasurer. The Treasurer may choose to use an outside agent to search for best available fares. When the Trustee submits the required information in a timely manner, effort will be made to accommodate arrival/departure time requests.

Travel to face-to-face meetings, unscheduled trips (not included in current year spending plan) and any other special trips require a spending plan. Spending plans are to be submitted to the Finance Committee for approval. Travel to and from GSO by supervisor(s) and Office Committee members do not require a spending plan.

Travel subject to reimbursement or other consideration will begin the minute the Trustee leaves their own environment and extends until they return to their own environment. Travel reimbursement will occur for the time spent conducting business for D.A./GSB. If personal time is combined with D.A. GSB business travel, the personal portion of travel will be at the Trustee's own expense.

Automobile Usage and Rental

Automobile rental may be necessary for certain approved travel. The number of Trustees requiring local ground transportation away from their home area will determine the number of cars rented. The D.A. GSB Chairperson will determine who will be the primary renter of each reimbursed car.

When auto travel is a personal choice over air travel, the lesser cost of the two will be reimbursed. If the Trustee is providing convenience, performing approved business, or eliminating the rental of an additional vehicle for D.A. GSB use, then the Finance Committee may decide to reimburse the auto traveler even though air travel would have cost less.

---

8   Approved by the GSB September 7, 2000.

Trustees using their own vehicle while conducting business for D.A. GSB will be reimbursed at the approved mileage rate in the current D.A. GSB Spending Plan or at the rate set by the Finance Committee. Tolls and parking fees will be reimbursed.

Air Travel

Air travel will be coordinated through the current Treasurer of D.A. GSB. The receipt from your airline must be turned over to the Treasurer as soon after your trip has ended as possible.

Ground transportation required to and from airport(s) will be reimbursed. Airport parking fees will be reimbursed.

Reimbursement for Personal Expenses Incurred While Traveling for D.A. GSB

Per Diem expenses are reimbursed contingent upon the performance of six (6) continuous hours of D.A. GSB business. Per Diem allowances can be used for meals and incidentals. The Finance Committee will determine a per diem for each trip. The established government rates will be considered, but not guaranteed. Travelers will be informed of the per diem rate prior to their trip. A travel form is provided to each traveler and must be submitted to the Finance Committee if reimbursement is expected.

Travel to Annual World Service Conference

The General Service Board pays for the expense of Trustees traveling to the Conference. This includes transportation, lodging, and meals beginning the evening before the D.A. GSB meeting, extending through the convocation.

GSB will cover an additional hotel night if a Trustee encounters schedule and airline conflicts. Such additional nights must be pre-approved by the Treasurer or the Chair of the D.A. GSB.

Cash Advance and Reimbursement Requests

When a cash advance has been granted, grantee is required to submit receipts immediately after the expenditure.

When a reimbursement request is made, receipts are to be attached to the Reimbursement Request Form.

Special Needs

The Executive Committee will consider special needs. The Executive Committee has the right to request special accommodations. Requests approved by the Executive Committee must then be approved by the Finance Committee. The additional cost of upgrades not approved by the Finance Committee will be paid for by the Trustee. This policy can be amended at the discretion of the Finance Committee or the Executive Committee; changes subject to approval of the GSB.

F. The Bylaws of Debtors Anonymous General Service Board, Inc.

Adopted September 1984[9]

Introduction

The Bylaws of the D.A. General Service Board are a legal document and cannot be suspended even with a unanimous vote, but can usually be amended with a vote of substantial unanimity. The bylaws cannot be in conflict with the Twelve Traditions, the D.A. Conference Charter, or the laws of the State of New York or the United States.

The Bylaws of Debtors Anonymous General Service Board, Inc.

The Trustees are subject to the laws of the State of New York and are expected to exercise the powers vested in them by law in a manner consonant with the faith that permeates and guides the

---

9   Revised 1989, August 2004, June 2008, September 28, 2008, December 14, 2008, May 19, 2009, December 15, 2009, Corrected Section 3.6 on January 23, 2010. Revised July 10, 2010, November 14, 2010, March 6, 2011, July 17, 2011, Feb 18, 2012, April 1, 2012, Jan 20, 2013, April 2015.

Fellowship, inspired by the Twelve Steps, in accordance with the Traditions, and in keeping with the Certificate and the bylaws.

Preamble

Debtors Anonymous General Service Board, Inc. (the 'Corporation') is formed to serve the Fellowship of Debtors Anonymous (the 'Fellowship'). It is a corporation created and designated by the Fellowship to maintain services for compulsive debtors who seek, through Debtors Anonymous ('D.A.'), the means to arrest the disease of compulsive debting through the application to their own lives of the Twelve Steps, adapted from the program of Alcoholics Anonymous, which constitute the recovery program upon which the Fellowship is founded.

These Twelve Steps are as follows:
1. We admitted we were powerless over debt—that our lives had become unmanageable.
2. Came to believe that a Power greater than ourselves could restore us to sanity.
3. Made a decision to turn our will and our lives over to the care of God as we understood Him.
4. Made a searching and fearless moral inventory of ourselves.
5. Admitted to God, to ourselves, and to another human being the exact nature of our wrongs.
6. Were entirely ready to have God remove all these defects of character.
7. Humbly ask Him to remove our shortcomings.
8. Made a list of all persons we had harmed and became willing to make amends to them all.
9. Made direct amends to such people wherever possible, except when to do so would injure them or others.
10. Continued to take personal inventory and when we were wrong promptly admitted it.
11. Sought through prayer and meditation to improve our conscious contact with God as we understood Him, praying only for knowledge of His will for us and the power to carry that out.
12. Having had a spiritual awakening as the result of these Steps, we tried to carry this message to compulsive debtors and to practice these principles in all our affairs.

The Twelve Steps and Twelve Traditions. Copyright © A.A. World Services, Inc.
Adapted and reprinted with permission.

The Corporation claims no proprietary right in the recovery program, for these Twelve Steps, like all spiritual truths, may now be regarded as available to all humanity. However, because these Twelve Steps have proven to constitute an effective spiritual basis for life which, if followed, arrests the disease of compulsive debting, the Corporation asserts the negative right of preventing, so far as it may be within its power to do so, any modification, alteration, or extension of these Twelve Steps as they are applied to the Fellowship, except at the insistence of the Fellowship. The corporation shall put forth its best efforts within the context of the Conference, articles of incorporation, and these bylaws to protect the Twelve Steps. The Corporation in its deliberations and decisions shall be guided by the Twelve Traditions of Debtors Anonymous (the 'Traditions'), which are as follows:
1. Our common welfare should come first; personal recovery depends on D.A. unity.
2. For our group purpose there is but one ultimate authority, a loving God as He may express Himself in our group conscience. Our leaders are but trusted servants; they do not govern.
3. The only requirement for D.A. membership is a desire to stop incurring unsecured debt.
4. Each group should be autonomous except in matters affecting other groups or D.A. as a whole.
5. Each group has but one primary purpose, to carry its message to the debtor who still suffers.

6. A D.A. group ought never endorse, finance, or lend the D.A. name to any related facility or outside enterprise lest problems of money, property, and prestige divert us from our primary purpose.

7. Every D.A. group ought to be fully self-supporting, declining outside contributions.

8. D.A. should remain forever nonprofessional, but our service centers may employ special workers.

9. D.A., as such, ought never to be organized; but we may create service boards or committees directly responsible to those they serve.

10. D.A. has no opinion on outside issues; hence the D.A. name ought never to be drawn into public controversy.

11. Our public relations policy is based on attraction rather than promotion; we need always maintain personal anonymity at the level of press, radio, and films.

12. Anonymity is the spiritual foundation of all our Traditions, ever reminding us to place principles before personalities.

The Twelve Steps and Twelve Traditions. Copyright © A.A. World Services, Inc. Adapted and reprinted with permission.

The Corporation shall use its best efforts to ensure that the Traditions are maintained, for the Corporation is regarded by the Fellowship as the custodian of the Traditions and, accordingly, the Corporation shall not itself nor, so far as it is within its power to do so, permit others to modify, alter, or amplify the Traditions, except in keeping with the provisions of the Certificate of Incorporation (the 'Certificate') and the bylaws of the Corporation (the 'bylaws'). The Corporation shall put forth its best efforts within the context of the Conference, Articles of Incorporation, and these bylaws to protect the Twelve Traditions.

The Twelve Concepts for D.A. World Service

Just as the Twelve Steps are guides for personal recovery and the Twelve Traditions are guides for group unity, the Twelve Concepts are guides for World Service. These Concepts serve as a path for Twelfth Step work on a world service level, and show how the D.A. groups, the World Service Conference, and the Debtors Anonymous General Service Board work together to carry recovery in D.A. to the still suffering debtor.

1. The ultimate responsibility and authority for Debtors Anonymous World Services should always remain with the collective conscience of our whole Fellowship as expressed through the D.A. groups.

2. The D.A. groups have delegated complete administrative and operational authority to the General Service Board. The groups have made the Conference the voice and conscience for the whole Fellowship, excepting for any change in the Twelve Steps, Twelve Traditions, and in Article 10, the General Warranties, of the Conference Charter.

3. As a traditional means of creating and maintaining a clearly defined working relationship between the groups, the World Service Conference, and the Debtors Anonymous General Service Board, it is suggested that we endow these elements of world service with a traditional "Right of Decision" in order to ensure effective leadership.

4. Throughout our Conference structure, we maintain at all levels a traditional "Right of Participation," ensuring a voting representation.

5. The traditional Rights of Appeals and Petition protect the minority opinion and ensure the consideration of personal grievances.

6. The Conference acknowledges the primary administrative responsibility of the Debtors Anonymous General Service Board.

7. The Conference recognizes that the Charter and the Bylaws of the Debtors Anonymous General Service Board serve as governing documents and that the Trustees have legal rights, while the rights of the Conference are spiritual, rooted in the Twelve Traditions. The

Concepts are not legal instruments.

8. The Debtors Anonymous General Service Board of Trustees assumes primary leadership for larger matters of overall policy, finance, and custodial oversight, and delegates authority for routine management of the General Service Office.

9. Good leaders, together with appropriate methods for choosing them at all levels, are necessary. At the world service level, the Board of Trustees assumes primary leadership for D.A. as a whole.

10. Every D.A. service responsibility should be equal to its service authority as defined by tradition, resolution, or D.A.'s Charter.

11. While the Trustees hold final authority for D.A. World Service administration, they will be assisted by the best possible staff members and consultants. Therefore, serious care and consideration will always be given to the compensation, selection, induction to service, rotation, and assignments for special rights and duties for all staff with a proper basis for determining financial compensation.

12. The Conference of Debtors Anonymous will observe the spirit of the Traditions, taking care not to become powerful and wealthy; having sufficient operating funds with a prudent reserve; having no authority over any other members; making important decisions by discussing and voting on issues wherever possible by substantial unanimity; not acting in a punitive way; not inciting public controversy; never performing any acts of government; and finally, always remaining democratic in thought and action.

Rev. 8/2004 D.A. World Service Conference (Concept 12)
Rev. 8/2005 D.A. World Service Conference (Concept 2)
Rev. 8/2006 D.A. World Service Conference (Concepts 5 & 6)

1. Offices

1.1 Principal Office.

The principal office of the Corporation shall be located in the Town of Woodstock, County of Ulster, State of New York.

1.2 Other Offices.

The Corporation may also have offices at such other places, both within and without the State of New York, as the General Service Board of Trustees may from time to time determine or the business of the Corporation may require.

2. Members

2.1 The Corporation shall have no members.

3.0 Trustees

3.1 Number, Composition and Qualification, Election, and Terms.

The business of the Corporation shall be managed by its General Service Board of Directors, which shall consist of a minimum of three (3) and a maximum of fifteen (15) Trustees, who shall be each at least eighteen years of age. Hereafter, throughout these Bylaws, the directors, so named to comply with the laws of the state of New York, shall be referred to as "Trustees." The number of Trustees may be changed by a majority vote of the entire General Service Board, provided that no decrease shall shorten the term of any incumbent Trustee. Trustees must be elected by a vote of substantial unanimity (as defined in section 7.7 of these Bylaws as a two-thirds majority) by the Board of Trustees. Except as hereafter otherwise provided, the election of Trustees must be ratified by a majority of all voting delegates in attendance at the annual D.A. World Service Conference. Upon ratification, a Trustee shall hold office for a term of three (3) years. Upon completion of a first three-year term, any Trustee who wishes to serve a second term must submit a letter of intent, be elected by substantial unanimity by the Board of Trustees, and be ratified by the next World Service Conference. If the maximum number of Trustees in a class (Class A or Class B) has been reached, a new Trustee in that class can be elected up to three (3) months before the next World Service Conference, when it is known that a Trustee currently serving in that class or region will be rotating off the Board. The incoming Trustee will attend that year's World Service Conference, begin serving on committees in the new conference year, and be ratified at that year's Convocation. (rev. 4/15, 6/18)

3.2 Composition and Qualification.

Trustees shall be divided into two categories: compulsive debtor Trustees and non-debtor Trustees. The compulsive debtors shall number a maximum of ten (10) and shall be referred to in these bylaws as Class A Trustees. Class A Trustees shall be persons who have arrested their compulsive debting, have not incurred new, unsecured debt for a period of three (3) consecutive years and who are living so far as possible within the concepts of the Twelve Steps which constitute the Debtors Anonymous recovery program.

The non-debtor Trustees shall number a maximum of five (5) and shall be referred to in these bylaws as Class B Trustees. Class B Trustees shall be persons who are not now and have not been afflicted by the disease of compulsive debting and who express a profound faith in the recovery program upon which the Fellowship is founded.

3.3 Terms of Class A and Class B Trustees

Class A Trustees shall be ineligible to serve for more than six (6) consecutive years, except in the case of a Class A Trustee serving as President (Chairperson), or Treasurer of the Corporation; a majority of the General Service Board may, having given due consideration to the spiritual principle of rotation of service, extend the period of eligibility for a maximum of one (1) consecutive year, if in the General Service Board's judgment this is in the best interest of the Corporation. [rev. 2/12, 8/20]

Class B Trustees shall be ineligible to serve for more than six (6) consecutive years, except in the case of a Class B Trustee serving as Treasurer of the Corporation; a majority of the General Service Board may, having given due consideration to the spiritual principle of rotation of service, extend the period of eligibility for a maximum of one (1) consecutive years if in the General Service Board's judgment this is in the best interest of the Corporation. [rev. 2/12, 8/20]

3.31 Rotation of Service Suggestion.

No former Trustee of the Debtors Anonymous General Service Board, upon completion of their board service, shall subsequently be invited to serve as Trustee or Appointed Committee Member. In the spirit of rotation of service, it is suggested that former trustees not serve as General Service Representative or Intergroup Service Representative. Furthermore, no trustee shall be employed by, or provide contracted services to, the Debtors Anonymous General Service Board for one year after their service as a trustee to the Debtors Anonymous General Service Board has ended. [rev. 06/08, 7/15]

3.4 Nomination and Election of Trustees

When seeking Trustee candidates to fill a vacancy, the General Service Board may solicit nominations from all interested parties. Candidates for Class A Trustee will whenever possible be drawn from D.A. members who have attended at least one D.A. World Service Conference as a group's General Service Representative or an Intergroup's Intergroup Service Representative. Candidates for Class B Trustee shall include but not be limited to recovering members of Alcoholics Anonymous. Except as hereafter otherwise provided, the election of Trustees must be ratified by a majority of all registered groups in attendance at the annual D.A. World Service Conference Convocation.

3.5 Regions

Previously, "Regions," in Section 3.5 in the Bylaws, referred to the number of Class A trustees that could serve on the GSB from a particular geographic location. In 2020, regional limits for Class A Trustees were eliminated. [rev. 07/11, 6/19, 2/20].

3.6 Newly Created Trusteeships and Vacancies.

Newly created trusteeships resulting from an increase in the number of Trustees or vacancies in the General Service Board of Trustees for any reason may be filled by a substantially unanimous vote of the Trustees then in office regardless of their number. A Trustee elected to fill a vacancy shall hold office until the next annual meeting at which the ratification of election of Trustees is in the regular order of business or until their successor is elected and qualified. Trustee terms begin upon ratification by the World Service Conference Convocation.

3.61 Trustee Leave of Absence

Trustees can take one (1) leave of absence per term of up to three (3) months for any reason. Notice of such leave must be submitted to the Chair via e-mail or first-class mail. Leave of absence will take effect upon receipt of such notice. Continued absence after three (3) months constitutes resignation from the GSB. [rev. 2/12]

3.7 Resignation and Removal of Trustee.

Any Trustee may resign from office at any time by delivering a written notice of resignation thirty (30) days in advance to the General Service Board of Trustees and the acceptance of the resignation, unless required by its terms, shall not be necessary to make such resignation effective. Any or all of the Trustees may be removed for cause by vote of the General Service Board of Trustees at any meeting, provided there is not less than a two-thirds quorum present at such meeting of Trustees at which such action is taken. Any Class A Trustee who incurs unsecured debt while serving as a Trustee is expected to resign immediately from the General Service Board. Incurring unsecured debt by a Class A Trustee is grounds for removal from the General Service Board of D.A. Other grounds for removal from the board may include unexplained or unexcused absences from board meetings or calls, disruptive or improper behavior, or failure to perform the duties of the position of Trustee.

Class A and Class B Trustees are expected, subject only to the laws of the State of New York and to these bylaws, at the request of the Conference of Debtors Anonymous, according to the provisions of the D.A. Charter, (that a three-quarter (3/4) vote of all Conference members present may bring about a reorganization of the General Service Board) to resign their trusteeships even though their terms of office as member Trustees may not have expired.

3.8 Indemnification.

The Corporation shall to the fullest extent permitted by law indemnify its Trustees and officers provided that no payment shall be made under this indemnity that would give rise to a tax under the Internal Revenue Code (rev. 2/08).

3.9 Insurance.

The Corporation is not required to purchase Directors' and Officers' liability insurance, but the Corporation may purchase such insurance if authorized and approved by the Board of Trustees. To the extent permitted by law, such insurance may insure the Corporation for any obligation it incurs as a result of these bylaws or operation of law and it may insure directly the Trustees, officers, employees, or volunteers of the Corporation for liabilities against which they are not entitled to indemnification under these bylaws.

[rev. 02/08, 03/11]

4.0 Conducting Business

4.1 Quorum and Manner of Acting.

A majority[10] of the entire General Service Board shall constitute a quorum for the transaction of

10   Rev. 20 January 2013.

business or of any specified item of business. Actions of the General Service Board of Trustees shall be authorized by substantial unanimity of the Trustees present at a meeting duly assembled at the time of the vote, if a quorum is present at such time, unless otherwise provided by the law or these bylaws. In the absence of a quorum, a majority of the Trustees present may adjourn any meeting to another time and place.

4.2 Action by the General Service Board of Trustees or Committee without a Meeting.

Any action required or permitted to be taken by the General Service Board of Trustees or by any committee of the General Service Board of Trustees may be taken without a meeting if all of the members of the General Service Board of Trustees or of such committee consent in writing to the adoption of a resolution authorizing the action. The resolution and the written consents thereto by the members of the General Service Board of Trustees of such committee shall be filed with the minutes of the proceedings of the General Service Board of Trustees or such committee. Communication via e-mail does not constitute a meeting. Decisions reached via e-mail by the General Service Board or its committees must be ratified at the next regularly scheduled meeting of the Board or committee.

4.3 Participation in General Service Board or Committee Meetings by Conference Telephone.

Any one or more Trustees or members of any committee of the General Service Board of Trustees may communicate by means of a conference telephone or similar communications equipment allowing all persons participating in the meeting to hear each other at the same time. Participation by such means shall constitute presence in person at such meeting.

4.4 Places of Meetings.

Meetings of the General Service Board of Trustees may be held at any place within or without the State of New York.

4.5 Annual and Regular Meetings.

Annual meetings of the General Service Board of Trustees and the World Service Conference Convocation, at which the election of officers and consideration of other matters takes place, shall be held within 90 days of the end of our fiscal year, or as soon thereafter as is practicable, or as determined by the General Service Board of Trustees and specified in the notice of a meeting as provided in section 4.7 of these bylaws. Regular meetings of the General Service Board of Trustees may be held without notice at such time and places as the General Service Board determines.

4.6 Special Meetings.

Special meetings of the General Service Board of Trustees may be called at any time, by any Trustee, upon written demand of not less than one-third (1/3) of the entire General Service Board or by the President (Chairperson).

4.7 Notice of Meetings; Waiver of Notice.

Notice of the time and place of each special meeting of the General Service Board of Trustees and of each annual meeting, shall be given to each Trustee by mailing it to them at their residence at least ten (10) days before the meeting or by telephoning, telegraphing, or emailing it to them at least seven (7) days before the meeting. Notice need not be given to any Trustee who submits a signed waiver of notice before or after a meeting or who attends the meeting without protesting the lack of notice to them. Notice of any adjourned meeting need not be given, other than by announcement at the meeting at which the adjournment is taken.

4.8 Compensation.

Trustees shall not receive compensation for their services, but the General Service Board of Trustees may authorize reimbursements of their reasonable out-of-pocket expenses in connection with the performance of their duties.

5.0 Committees

5.1 Executive Committee and Standing Committees.

The General Service Board of Trustees by resolution adopted by a majority of the entire General Service Board, may designate an Executive Committee or other standing committees, each consisting of three (3) or more Trustees. The Executive Committee and other standing committees shall serve at the pleasure of the General Service Board of Trustees. All actions of the Executive Committee and other standing committees shall be reported to the General Service Board of Trustees at the General Service Board of Trustees next meeting. The Executive Committee shall have all the authority of the General Service Board of Trustees, except as otherwise provided in such resolution or by law. Other standing committees shall have such authority as provided by resolution or by law. The Executive Committee and such other standing committees shall adopt rules of procedure as outlined by Robert's Rules of Order and shall meet as provided by those rules or by Resolutions of the General Service Board of Trustees. The General Service Board of Trustees shall have the power at any time to fill vacancies in, to change the membership of, or to discharge such committees.

5.2 Other Committees.

The General Service Board of Trustees, by resolution adopted by a majority of the entire General Service Board, may create special committees as deemed desirable, each consisting of Trustees and appointed committee members, to serve at the General Service Board of Trustees' pleasure, with such powers and duties as the General Service Board of Trustees determines, subject to any limitation in law.

6.0 Officers

6.1 Number, Security.

The executive officers of the Corporation shall be President (Chairperson), one or more Vice Presidents (Vice Chairpersons), a Secretary, and a Treasurer. Any two or more offices may be held by the same person, except the offices of President/Chairperson and Secretary. The General Service Board of Trustees may require any officer to give security for the faithful performance of their duties.

6.2 Election, Term of Office.

The executive officers of the Corporation shall be elected annually by the General Service Board of Trustees and ratified by the World Service Conference Convocation. Candidates for each office shall submit a letter of intent and nomination materials to the General Service Board Nominations Committee at least 120 days before the annual meeting of the General Service Board. Each officer shall hold office until the end of the next annual meeting of the General Service Board of Trustees or, if the office is being vacated before the end of the term, until the election and qualification of their successor. The President (Chairperson) and Treasurer will both be expected to serve a two (2) year term and to train their successors during the second year. No Trustee shall serve more than four (4) years in the same office. (rev. 4/15)

6.3 Subordinate Officers.

The General Service Board of Trustees may elect subordinate officers (including assistant Treasurers and assistant Secretaries) as it may deem proper, each of whom shall hold office for such period and have such powers and duties as the General Service Board of Trustees determines.

6.4 Resignation and Removal of Officers.

Any officer may resign at any time by delivering a written notice of resignation 30 days in advance to the General Service Board of Trustees. Any officer elected or appointed by the General Service

Board of Trustees may be removed by the General Service Board of Trustees, with or without cause.

6.5 Vacancies.

A vacancy in any office may be filled for the unexpired term by the General Service Board of Trustees.

6.6 The President (Chairperson).

The President (Chairperson) shall be the chief executive officer of the Corporation and shall preside at all meetings of the General Service Board of Trustees, provided, however, that she/he may assign such duty to another Trustee. Subject to the control of the General Service Board of Trustees, she/he shall generally supervise the business of the Corporation and shall have such other power and duties as presidents of corporations usually have or as the General Service Board assigns to them. The President/Chairperson will be expected to serve a two (2) year term and train their successor during the second year. A Trustee may serve as President for no more than four (4) consecutive years unless a majority of the General Service Board vote to extend the period of eligibility for not more than two years. By tradition, the office of President (Chairperson) is held by a Class A Trustee.

6.7 The Vice President.

Each Vice President (Vice Chairperson) shall have such powers and perform such duties as the General Service Board of Trustees or the President may from time to time assign to them. During the President's (Chairperson's) second year in office, the Vice President will receive training from the President, in preparation for becoming President the following year. A Trustee may serve as Vice President for no more than four (4) consecutive years, unless a majority of the General Service Board vote to extend the period of eligibility for not more than one year.

6.8 The Treasurer.

The Treasurer shall be the chief financial officer of the Corporation and shall be in charge of the Corporation's financial books and accounts. Subject to the control of the General Service Board of Trustees, she/he shall have such powers and perform such other duties as the General Service Board of Trustees or the President (Chairperson) may from time to time assign to them. The Treasurer will be expected to serve a term of at least two (2) years, and to train their successor. A Trustee may serve as Treasurer for no more than four (4) consecutive years, unless a majority of the General Service Board vote to extend the period of eligibility for not more than one year.

6.9 The Secretary.

The Secretary shall be secretary of, and keep the minutes of, all meetings of the General Service Board of Trustees, shall be responsible for giving notice of all meetings of the General Service Board of Trustees, shall maintain custody of the corporate seal and apply it to any instrument requiring it. Subject to the control of the General Service Board of Trustees, she/he shall have such other powers and perform such other duties as the General Service Board of Trustees or President may from time to time assign her/him. In the absence of the Secretary from any meeting, the minutes shall be kept by the person appointed for that purpose by the presiding officer. A Trustee may serve as Secretary for no more than four (4) consecutive years, unless a majority of the General Service Board vote to extend the period of eligibility for not more than one year.

6.10 The Assistant Treasurer.

The Assistant Treasurer shall assist the Treasurer as required. During the Treasurer's final year in office, the Assistant Treasurer will receive training from the Treasurer, in preparation for becoming the next Treasurer.

7.0 Miscellaneous.

7.1 Seal.

The General Service Board of Trustees shall adopt a corporate seal, which shall be in the form of a circle and shall bear the Corporations name and the year and state in which it was incorporated.

7.2 Fiscal Year.

The fiscal year of the Corporation shall begin on the first day of July in each year and shall end on the thirtieth day of June next following, unless otherwise determined by the General Service Board.

7.3 Contracts, Checks, Bank Accounts.

The funds of the Corporation shall be deposited in the Corporation's name with such banks, trust companies, or other depositories as the General Service Board of Trustees may designate. The General Service Board of Trustees shall determine who shall be authorized from time to time to sign checks, drafts, or other orders for the payment of money, acceptances, notes or other evidences of indebtedness, to enter into contracts or to execute and deliver other documents and instruments.

7.4 Annual Reports.

The General Service Board of Trustees shall direct the President and Treasurer of the Corporation to present at each annual meeting of the General Service Board of Trustees a financial report in accordance with paragraph (a) of Section 519 of the Not-For-Profit Corporation Law of the State of New York but omitting the requirements of subparagraph (5) of said paragraph (a) of Section 519.

7.5 Amendments.

These bylaws may be amended, added to, rescinded, or repealed at a meeting by two-thirds of the entire General Service Board, except that any amendment which changes or strikes any provision specifying the quorum requirements or the proportion of votes necessary for the transaction of business or any specified item of business must be authorized by a vote of three-quarters (3/4) of the entire General Service Board of Trustees.

7.6 Definition of 'Entire Board.'

As used in these bylaws, the term 'entire Board' means the total number of Trustees which the Corporation would have if there were no vacancies on the Board of Trustees. [11]

7.7 Definition of 'Substantial Unanimity.'

As used in these bylaws, the term 'substantial unanimity' means a two-thirds majority of the current Trustees voting. [12]

7.8 Definition of "Appointed Committee Member"

As used in these Bylaws, the term "Appointed Committee Member" ("ACM") means a non-trustee D.A. member who is selected to serve on a GSB committee. ACMs are not members of the General Service Board of Trustees and do not participate in GSB meetings. However, they are voting members of the committee on which they serve. ACMs serve three-year terms that are renewed annually, for a maximum of two three-year terms. An ACM candidate is elected if he or she receives a unanimous vote of the GSB committee seeking an ACM, followed by a vote of substantial unanimity by the General Service Board of Trustees. Furthermore, no ACM shall be employed by, or provide contracted services to, the Debtors Anonymous General Service Board for one year after their service as an ACM to the Debtors Anonymous General Service Board has ended. [rev. 7/15]

---

11   To bring bylaws in line with sec 712 of NY Not-for-profit Corporation Law, this text replaces "As used in these by-laws, the term 'entire Board' means the total number of Trustees entitled to vote." Change made Nov 14, 2010.

12   Text replaced "As used in these bylaws, the term 'substantial unanimity' means a two-thirds majority of the entire Board of Trustees entitled to vote." Changed Nov 14, 2010.

CHAPTER 10 – THE GENERAL SERVICE OFFICE

Text from the GSO pamphlet, reprinted here at the request of the 2003 World Service Conference. All rights reserved. Note: Revisions were made in 2006 and 2008 to update the information.

GSO

General Service Office of Debtors Anonymous

GSO Mission Statement

The mission of the Debtors Anonymous General Service Office is to provide timely consistent service and D.A. information to suffering debtors, D.A. groups, and other interested parties. Using the spiritual principles of the 12 Steps and 12 Traditions, the General Service Office facilitates communication and unity within D.A. and meets the challenges of a growing fellowship with professionalism and compassion.

What Is the GSO?

The General Service Office (GSO) is the administrative "heart" of Debtors Anonymous (D.A.), carrying out D.A.'s primary purpose—to carry the message to the still-suffering compulsive debtor—every day. It is the hub of day-to-day communication with the suffering newcomer, with D.A. members and groups, between the groups and the General Service Board, with the media, and with the larger world. Special workers, acting within the D.A. Traditions and guided by the D.A. Concepts of Service, serve a growing number of groups and members around the world.

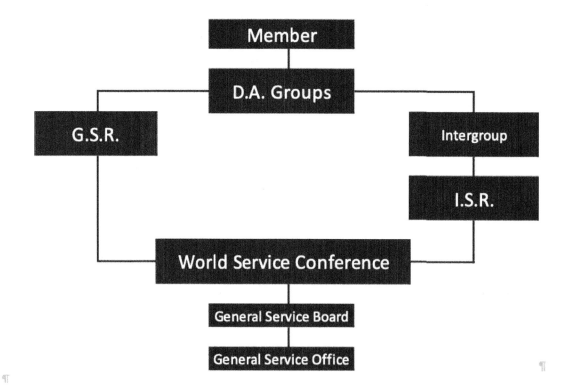

What Does the GSO Do?

The GSO carries out the same functions as those of any main office or headquarters of a nonprofit organization; however, it does much more because of its unique role of service to the compulsive debtor:

Service to Newcomers and Members

The GSO is the primary point of contact for many newcomers and members. It responds to a rapidly growing number of letters, phone calls, faxes, and email messages each week. Our service workers answer questions, provide meeting locations, explain the basics of D.A. to all who need help, and sometimes, just lend an understanding ear to the troubled. The GSO maintains and continuously updates a complete database of D.A. meetings worldwide and on the Internet. It monitors the D.A. website (www.debtorsanonymous.org), working with the General Service Board Information Technology Committee, the World Service Conference, and contracted professional service firms.

Literature Distribution Service

The GSO administers the publication and distribution of all D.A. literature, including pamphlets, books, audiotapes, guides, compact discs, and Web-based materials. It receives and processes all literature/media orders from individuals, groups, Intergroups, distributors, and the public to spread the D.A. message.

Service to Groups and Intergroups

The GSO is the focal point of contact between groups and Intergroups and the General Service Board (GSB) between World Conferences. It administers and distributes the *DA Focus*, the official GSB service newsletter, and formal letters to the Fellowship from the Board. It also distributes the Debtors Anonymous World Service Conference Report to all groups and Intergroups. Our service workers either respond to or refer to the proper Trustee inquiries from groups and Intergroups.

Service to the World Conference

The primary responsibility of managing the annual World Conference rests with the sponsor city's Host Committee and the Conference Committee. However, the GSO helps coordinate the annual World Conference with administrative tasks before, after, and between conferences.

Service to the Media and the Professional Community

Working with the Public Information Committee and Trustee Liaison, the GSO responds to requests from the news media and from outside professionals, such as therapists, counselors, judicial systems, and financial consultants, for information about D.A. and the disease of compulsive debting.

Service to the General Service Board of Trustees (GSB) and its Committees

The General Service Board of Trustees, Inc. is responsible for putting into practice D.A.'s group conscience as expressed through the will of the World Conference. The Board also fulfills all fiduciary responsibilities required of nonprofit corporations by law; the Trustees have serious legal duties that they perform, such as protecting copyrights and service marks and filing required forms and tax returns. The GSO assists the GSB and its committees in carrying out these responsibilities.

Structure of the GSB

The GSB may consist of up to 15 Trustees, up to 10 recovering debtors and up to 5 non-debtors. Each year it elects a Chair, a Vice-Chair, a Treasurer, and a Secretary. It has a number of committees that both carry out the wishes of the World Conference and develop new projects to benefit the Fellowship. The committees include Executive, Finance, Office, Nominations and Procedures, Literature, Long-Range Planning, Communications and Technology, Audit and Legal Affairs, Literature Translations and Licensing, and International. A Trustee also serves as a Liaison to one of the ten World Conference Committees: Business Debtors Anonymous, Conference, Hospitals, Institutions and Prisons, Internal Operations (GSO), International, Resource Development, Fellowship Communications, Public Information, Information Technology, and Literature. Trustees also act as liaisons to informal caucuses that represent the interests of Intergroups, Spiritually Sustainable Earning, and Underserved and Under-represented Outreach.

What Can You and Your Group Do for the GSO?

As a D.A. member, General Service Representative (GSR), Intergroup Service Representative (ISR), or group or Intergroup officer, you can help the GSO—and the still-suffering compulsive debtor—in many ways:

- Share your experience, strength, and hope. Your email messages, phone calls, and letters help the GSO and the GSB stay in touch with and respond to your and your group's true needs.

- Keep the GSO informed of changes. You, your group GSR, your ISR, or your group officers need to help make sure that the D.A. database includes accurate, up-to-date information about your group (meeting days, locations, and times, contact persons, and GSR). You can keep the GSO informed about your Intergroups and Area Groups (a group of GSRs in your area) and let the GSO know about special events that could be posted on the D.A. website.

Remember our Seventh Tradition

Just like your own group, the GSO is self-supporting through the contributions of D.A. groups and members everywhere. The GSO cannot serve you or any suffering compulsive debtor without your personal and your group's experience, strength, hope, and financial support.

The GSO must serve a rapidly growing number of members like you and groups like yours, and it cannot do so without adequate funds and prudent reserves. Each D.A. member and each group is asked to provide regular support at every level so each D.A. member, each group, and the GSO can do the most important task that any of us has: To carry the message to the still-suffering compulsive debtor.

Suggested Contribution Plan

Here is a suggested plan for group and individual contributions:

Group Contributions

- Establish a group spending plan and local treasury with adequate prudent reserves, usually three months of normal expenses.

- Meet your local expenses first to keep the meeting healthy.

- Divide any surplus—each month—by the following recommended formula:

  □ If your area has an Intergroup, contribute 50% of any surplus to Intergroup and 50% to the GSB

  □ If your area has an Intergroup and an Area Group of GSRs, then contribute 45% to Intergroup, 45% to the G.S.B, and 10% to the Area Group.

  □ If your area does NOT have either an Intergroup or an Area Group, contribute 100% of the surplus to the GSB

- Intergroups and Area Groups, in turn, are asked to contribute 100% of their surpluses, if any, to the GSB.

- Groups, Intergroups, and Area Groups may make unlimited donations to the GSB each year.

- Each Treasurer should send a contribution by check, money order, or by online donation or Bill Pay after the group's monthly business meeting.

- Special Event Collections for GSB: Many groups and Intergroups pass a special basket to support the GSB during special events, such as Fellowship Days, World Service Month (to celebrate D.A.'s anniversary each year), Group Anniversaries, and the like.

Individual Contributions

- Double Your Dollar: Each individual D.A. member who is able is asked to contribute $2 per meeting so your local group has enough funds to pay rent, buy literature, sponsor special events, build a prudent reserve, and contribute to any Area Group, any Intergroup, and the GSB.

- Even if you are unable to give, please keep coming back. The still-suffering compulsive debtor is the most important person in D.A., and all of the efforts of both the GSO and the GSB serve you and help you and all compulsive debtors like you recover.

- Thrive With Five: Members who have experienced prosperity through recovery in D.A. are asked to put $5 in the basket at each meeting.

- Individuals can make separate contributions to the GSB of up to $12,000 per year. Individuals may want to give directly to the GSB on a regular basis or to celebrate special occasions, such as...

- Prosperity Contributions: If you receive a new job or a raise, pay off a debt, resolve a legal issue successfully, or are blessed in any other way through your recovery in D.A., you may want to express your gratitude with a contribution.

- Anniversary Gifts: Many D.A. members give special gifts to the GSB to commemorate the anniversary of their first D.A. meeting or their first day of not incurring unsecured debt. Some give an amount equal to the number of anniversaries (for example, $10 for 10 years in the program) while others give some multiple of that amount (for example, $50, $5 for each year for 10 years).

- World Service Month: Many members and groups make special donations during World Service Month in April each year to honor D.A.'s anniversary and its success in helping the suffering compulsive debtor. You may wish to consider giving an amount equal to the number of D.A. anniversaries.

- Regular Contributions: Many D.A. members put monthly or quarterly contributions to the GSB, above and beyond their group donations, in their personal spending plans.

- NOTE: Remember that all individual contributions to the General Service Board are tax deductible for United States residents to the maximum extent allowable by U.S. law. For members residing outside the U.S., please check your local tax laws.

Mail contributions (check or money order) to:

Debtors Anonymous
P.O. Box 920888
Needham, MA 02492-0009

tel.: 781-453-2743 | in the U.S. 800-421-2383
email: office@debtorsanonymous.org
http://www.debtorsanonymous.org

CHAPTER 11 – *WAYS & MEANS*® AND THE *DA FOCUS*

A. Ways & Means®

Ways & Means, an electronic meeting in print for the Fellowship of Debtors Anonymous, is published quarterly by the D.A. General Service Board, and is posted on the D.A. website, www.debtorsanonymous.org. It is a forum for sharing the experience, strength, and hope of D.A. members, groups, and other service bodies. Articles represent the viewpoints of their authors and are not intended to be statements of D.A. policy, nor does publication constitute or imply endorsement by D.A. as a whole, the D.A. General Service Board, or the *Ways & Means*.

Before the first publication of *Ways & Means* in 1988, the desire for a newsletter to carry the D.A. message and facilitate communication within the Fellowship went back several years. D.A.'s first two regional newsletters, New York's The Bottom Line and Southern California's Checks & Balances, first saw print in the early 1980s. Checks & Balances has been published continuously ever since, and The Bottom Line was recently revived after a three-year hiatus.

D.A.'s first national publication, entitled The Newsletter to the Groups, came out with its first edition in 1986. Published monthly, it was written in letter form as a communication from the GSB, with the idea that it would be read to members by an officer of each group. The founding editor, a GSB Trustee with writing experience, was frustrated when officers did not follow this plan, but rather distributed it for individual reading.

After experimenting with this format for two years, the General Service Board decided to create a true newsletter format, and named it *Ways & Means*, reflecting the efforts of D.A. members to share the "ways and means" by which they lived the D.A. Program prosperously and with integrity without incurring any unsecured debt. It was published six times a year from 1988 through the early 1990s but increasing costs and a lack of articles later reduced this to four times per year.

Numerous attempts to make *Ways & Means* self-supporting through subscription income were unsuccessful for nearly two decades. Despite many promotions and circulation-building efforts, paid circulation never exceeded 300. At the 2001 World Service Conference in Baltimore, the Fellowship came close to discontinuing the newsletter. But the Conference granted a one-year reprieve, and efforts by supporters of the newsletter were rewarded with plans for a new form of publication.

Beginning in 2004, an electronic version, posted on the D.A. website, was produced alongside the print version. This tandem production continued until all the subscription obligations for the print newsletter were fulfilled in 2007. Since then, *Ways & Means* has been produced only for the website.

Internet statistics indicate *Ways & Means* is one of the most popular features of the website, with each issue having several times the circulation of the former print publication. Several D.A. groups now have "*Ways & Means*" meetings and download many copies for use as readings during the meeting. Back issues of *Ways & Means* for the past several years are also available on the website.

Since becoming an electronic publication, *Ways & Means* has dramatically expanded. From a standard size of 4 to 7 pages during the print years, the average size is now 10 to 14 pages. A 16-page issue, the largest in its history, was published in 2009. In 2018, the GSB voted to designate *Ways & Means* as a "magazine" rather than a "newsletter."

Editing and layout for *Ways & Means* are done by the Communications Committee of the D.A. General Service Board. As the Fellowship's "meeting in print" with the blessing of past WSCs, *Ways & Means* has "conceptual approval" to be distributed at D.A. meetings and through the D.A. website. (Since a quarterly publication cannot come before the annual World Service Conference for approval under the regular Literature Approval Process, the process of conceptual approval makes it approved for use under all D.A. circumstances.)

Submissions from readers on any aspect of the D.A. recovery program or issues related to D.A. as a Fellowship are welcome. If chosen, submissions become the property of the Debtors Anonymous General Service Board and will not be returned. As with all D.A. publications, everyone submitting writing, artwork, or other creative work will be required to sign a standard publishing release form granting rights to the work to D.A. and releasing D.A. from legal liability. Those submitting work to *Ways & Means* automatically acknowledge that they will not receive compensation for their work, and that the work may be viewed by an unknown number of readers in unknown locations.

Submissions can be made by email to communications@debtorsanonymous.org or in hard copy form by mail to:

Ways & Means
c/o D.A. General Service Office
PO Box 920888
Needham, Mass 02492

The author's full name and mailing address, phone number, and email address should be included with the submission. (This information will be kept confidential.) Story ideas and questions should be sent to the same addresses.

B. DA Focus

The *DA Focus* is the GSB's quarterly report to the Fellowship of D.A., reflecting the activities of the D.A. General Service Board and World Service Conference. It includes details on service-related occurrences and events, primarily at the World Service level, updates throughout the year on the work of GSB and WSC committees, and financial reports for D.A.

Prior to 1997, the General Service Board had used the only national newsletter, *Ways & Means*, as its primary means of communicating its news to the Fellowship. However, at the 1995 World Service Conference, the Conference voted to separate what had been *Ways & Means* into two newsletters, with two distinct functions.

The division occurred at the beginning of 1997, with *Ways & Means* becoming the vehicle for D.A. members and groups to write about their personal recovery and their views on recovery and service issues. A new newsletter, the GSB Quarterly News (subtitled A Quarterly Communication between the General Service Board and Fellowship of D.A.), debuted in January 1997, featuring news of GSB activities and viewpoints to D.A. as a whole.

In June 1999, the GSB Quarterly News was renamed Board Call (with the same subtitle), a name it retained until the fall of 2004, when it was again renamed the *DA Focus,* a name it retains today, although the subtitle has changed slightly to The Quarterly World Service Newsletter For The Fellowship Of Debtors Anonymous.

The *DA Focus,* which usually runs eight pages but has occasionally been longer, is also published by the Communications Committee of the GSB. As the voice of the General Service Board, it does not accept submissions from the Fellowship at large, which are always welcome in *Ways & Means*. For several years now, both the current and back issues of the *DA Focus* are also available for viewing or download from the D.A. website.

CHAPTER 12 – THOUGHTS ON THE TWELVE CONCEPTS FOR WORLD SERVICE

Concept 1

The ultimate responsibility and authority for Debtors Anonymous World Services should always remain with the collective conscience of our whole Fellowship as expressed through the D.A. groups.

This Concept recognizes the fundamental fact that all authority in D.A. flows through the groups and their members. As the Second Tradition recognizes, the ultimate authority in D.A. is a loving God as expressed in our group conscience. The groups are the primary interpreters and discerners of the Higher Power's will for the future of D.A. They remain at the top of the "inverted triangle" which represents the D.A. service structure. It is they who select the general service representatives (GSRs) and who create the Intergroups represented by Intergroup service representatives (ISRs) who attend the annual World Service Conference. The groups retain the power to discipline all elements of D.A. service through their control of D.A.'s finances. Since D.A. is constrained by the Seventh Tradition from seeking outside funding, ultimately the groups provide the source of D.A.'s income, either directly through group contributions or indirectly through group purchases of literature.

It is because the groups retain this ultimate authority that the positions of GSR and ISR are so important in D.A. It becomes necessary that a communications link exist to express that authority, and the GSRs and ISRs are that link. In consequence, it becomes vital for the GSRs to listen carefully to their individual group members and the conscience of the group as a whole as expressed at business meetings. Only if GSRs or ISRs are informed of the group conscience can they carry that understanding beyond the group level to the World Service Conference. It is equally important that these representatives ensure that their groups are fully informed of the facts upon which these decisions are based. Thus, it is their responsibility to report back to the members all information relevant to the World Service structure.

The groups cannot exercise this responsibility and authority by themselves. They must act through the World Service Conference, composed of GSRs, ISRs, Trustees, and appropriate office staff.

The watchword for this Concept is responsibility. Groups and their members must act responsibly in learning about issues that affect D.A. as a whole and in exploring the possibilities for D.A.'s future. Often groups resist providing adequate time to their GSR to report back on matters of general importance. This is one of the most obvious ways in which groups disregard Concept One through lack of awareness. Responsibility to keep the group informed also rests upon the GSR or ISR. Information flows both ways via the GSR or ISR. It is that person's duty to represent the group and attempt to express its conscience. If GSRs fail to recognize their responsibility to discern the group conscience, they are tempted to act as if they are the ultimate arbiters, failing to consult and listen. Equally important, the GSR has the obligation to report back to the group on their decisions and votes and to accept criticism gracefully if there has been a failure to listen.

Concept 2

The D.A. groups have delegated complete administrative and operational authority to the General Service Board. The groups have made the Conference the voice and conscience for the whole Fellowship, excepting for any change in the Twelve Steps, Twelve Traditions, and in Article 10, the General Warranties, of the Conference Charter.

The idea of trust is basic to this Concept. It informs us that the groups have made the decision to place their trust in the World Service Conference and the General Service Board (GSB) to make the best decisions for the Fellowship in all matters of administration and operation of D.A. The Second Tradition points out that our leaders are "trusted servants." They do not order or direct groups or their members. Instead, they are to listen to and try to carry out the will of the groups, receiving the trust of its members to discern the best ways—within the context of the Steps, Traditions, and Concepts—to implement that will. Under this Concept, the General Service Board, members of which are known as Trustees, is given great freedom and flexibility in carrying out the business of the D.A. Fellowship. The Board has the corresponding obligation to act carefully and prudently.

It is obvious that, in most matters, the groups can directly exercise neither policy-making nor operational authority in implementing the group conscience. Because of this, Concept Two maintains that the groups must act through the Conference, which they have made the voice and conscience of the whole Fellowship. This Concept thus establishes trust of the Conference to act in a way that represents the informed opinions of the groups and their members.

As Concept Eight states, primary leadership in overall policy matters rests with the General Service Board. However, leadership that acts without listening to advice is neither wise nor prudent. Since the Conference is the collective voice and conscience of the Fellowship, the Board has an obligation to listen to and to heed that advice, in all but the most extreme cases. (For example, when the Conference adopted a motion to direct how outside literature should be used at meetings, the GSB refused to implement this directive on the ground that it violated several Traditions.) In general, duty calls whenever the Conference acts with substantial unanimity, that is, by a two-thirds vote. Even in those cases where the Conference is unable to muster a two-thirds vote for a course of action, the General Service Board has the duty to listen to the opinions expressed and, in appropriate cases, to moderate or change course to reflect what has been discussed.

In three areas, however, the groups have retained their authority over the Conference and General Service Board. These matters are regarded as so basic to the D.A. program of recovery, to D.A. unity, and to the effectiveness of service that no action should be taken without the expressed consent of the groups. These three areas are changes to the Twelve Steps, the Twelve Traditions, and Article 10 (the General Warranties) of the Conference Charter. Here, the Conference Charter recognizes that the World Service Conference may not act to change these fundamental principles unless three-quarters of the D.A. groups grant their permission to do so.

Concept 3

As a traditional means of creating and maintaining a clearly defined working relationship between the groups, the World Service Conference, and the Debtors Anonymous General Service Board, it is suggested that we endow these elements of world service with a traditional "Right of Decision" in order to ensure effective leadership.

The "Right of Decision" refers to the right of every person in service to act in accordance with their best understanding of the will of the Higher Power in carrying out assigned duties. Except in the most extreme cases, such as a paid General Service Office employee refusing to carry out the direct instructions of the GSB, each member of D.A. is answerable to their own conscience. Again, the ideal of "trusting our trusted servants" plays a role.

Even more important in understanding this Concept is the idea of honesty. The Right of Decision can be exercised only in the context of a true dedication to honesty in all things. Each person seeking to exercise this right must perform a thorough examination of conscience and an honest evaluation of motive. All too often, what seems at first glance like a prompting of principle turns out to be an exercise in rationalization. Motives such as pride or anger can be disguised in the cloak of this Concept. Sometimes our character defects like sloth or a desire to please prompt our actions.

The Right of Decision is exercised most frequently by the GSR or ISR. A GSR who has actively sought out the conscience of the group and who comes to the Conference with a clear idea of what the group wants may be presented with new facts or arguments that did not occur to the group's members in their discussion. The GSR may learn of needs of other groups or regions of the country or world that the group did not consider. In such a case, the GSR may appropriately exercise the Right of Decision to reach a conclusion different from that of the group and vote contrary to the group's direction. In doing so, the person exercising that right must be prepared to justify their actions to the group.

However, the right applies to all levels of service. Thus a group officer has the Right of Decision in carrying out the functions of the office she or he occupies. At the most mundane level, the group setup person has the right to choose the cookies to be served. At a more important level, the group Chair has both the duty and right to prevent an individual from disrupting a meeting in progress. In each case, the decision maker must operate within the constraints of delegated authority: if the group has determined that chocolate cookies must be served, the setup person cannot choose to serve lemon cookies; the Chair cannot ban an individual from group meetings without consulting both the group and the Third Tradition.

Similarly, a Trustee who has attended the Conference and voted in favor of a motion may find, upon further consideration, that the needs of D.A. would be seriously undermined if the motion were implemented. Facts later discovered may make a course of conduct appear harmful to the Fellowship. Or, the same Trustee may have voted against the motion and continue to conclude that its implementation would violate a Tradition or Concept of World Service. In such cases, the Trustee would be free to refuse implementation. In that event, the Trustee, and the whole Board if it agrees with them, should be prepared to explain and justify the decision.

This duty to report back to the group is extremely valuable in ensuring that the Right of Decision is exercised appropriately. The person who seeks to invoke this principle should always consider the report that must be rendered and the duty of accountability.

In the end, the Right of Decision provides insurance against the dangers of micromanagement and second-guessing. When an individual has been entrusted with the authority to perform a function, he or she should ordinarily be able to act without fear of unjustified criticism because someone else might have decided differently. While acting within the scope of this authority, one should reasonably expect to be allowed to act as seems fit. Honest decision making should never be condemned, if it is done with care, consideration, and prudence.

Concept 4

Throughout our Conference structure, we maintain at all levels a traditional "Right of Participation," ensuring a voting representation.

One of the fundamental principles in D.A. service is the ideal of equality. To the extent possible in carrying out D.A.'s business, we try to emphasize the basic dignity and inherent worth of every individual. This emphasis on equality underlies both the Fourth and the Fifth Concepts.

As a result, we attempt to ensure that everyone in service—from the groups down to the General Service Board—is accorded the right to participate in the decisional process in a way commensurate with their authority and duties. Thus, every group member—and a person is a member if he or she says so—has the right to participate in group business meetings and has a vote equal to that of any other member. If the group has a steering committee, in the steering committee each member of that committee must be consulted and heard whenever possible before a decision is made.

On the Intergroup level, Intergroup Representatives must be consulted at the monthly or quarterly meetings before any major decision is taken or policy change is implemented. This means that meetings must be scheduled at a time and place that is most convenient to the greatest number of representatives, and with sufficient notice to all.

At the World Service Conference, limited time makes it difficult for all who wish to speak to be heard. However, efforts must be made to provide an opportunity for a representative cross-section of the delegates and Trustees present to speak their minds. In D.A. we should be careful not to abuse tactics available in rules of order, such as calling the question, to prevent a full opportunity for all relevant viewpoints to be heard. In all important matters, time rules should be flexible enough to enable the greatest number of GSRs and ISRs to present their arguments. Here it is also important to note that the Office Manager of the General Service Office (GSO) has been given a voice and a vote at the Conference because the experience of that person may be helpful in the decisional process and because that person is the one who will most likely have to answer for Conference decisions.

In meetings of the General Service Board, each member is given an opportunity to speak. Their opinion is of equal weight with that of any other Trustee. While the views of an officer may be enlightening in matters affecting that office, and while committee members may have greater expertise on a particular issue relevant to their committee, this special knowledge can never be decisive. All decisions in D.A. should be made only after full participation by all parties.

Finally, the Right of Participation should be viewed as a right of meaningful participation. Each opinion should be accorded the deference and respect that we would want to be given to our own opinions. The fact that a person is perceived as negative or even obstructive should not cause us to close our ears to their comments. Even the person we most dislike may be used by the Higher Power to speak the truth if we are willing to listen. We should never be dismissive of any person's contribution to the debate, if we wish to carry out the intent of this Concept.

Concept 5

The traditional Rights of Appeal and Petition protect the minority opinion and ensure the consideration of personal grievances.

Concept Five deals with two related rights: "Appeal" and "Petition." Both are based upon the principle of the equality of all persons involved in service. Even more important, both require courage and a willingness to respect the opinions of a minority. Both involve the recognition that the majority view may be wrong, and that the minority may be articulating the voice of the Higher Power in D.A.'s affairs. Each requires that the majority have the humility to be willing to recognize its own fallibility.

The Right of Appeal refers to the duty of the majority to listen to the minority viewpoint in any debate on issues of importance to D.A. Most frequently, it comes into play after a vote is taken. Whenever there are "no" votes, the Chair should always ask if there is a minority opinion that wishes to be heard. If, as a matter of honestly held principle, a person in the minority believes that the majority has made a serious mistake of principle or fact, that person should rise to restate their position for consideration by the majority. Such a power to delay and confuse debate should never be exercised without careful thought. The minority member should never be acting out of hurt feelings or wounded pride, but only out of a deeply held conviction that the decision just reached may seriously harm the D.A. group.

When a member of the minority in D.A. does so, he or she is said to be exercising the Right of Appeal. At that point, the Chair should then ask if anyone who voted with the majority wishes to change their mind. If someone is so willing, that person should make a motion to reconsider. If the motion is seconded, a vote will be taken on whether the body wishes to reconsider. If a majority votes to reconsider, then debate on the original question reopens.

This Right of Appeal is of immense spiritual importance. It requires great humility on the part of a majority to recognize that it may have erred. It requires great courage on the part of a member to face down the majority and call it to recognize its duties. And it requires a great degree of respect for the rights of all members to implement this right.

In practice, the Right of Appeal is exercised at the World Service Conference to great effect. At each Conference there will usually be one or two instances in which a member of the minority calls the majority to task for its actions. And, in about half of these cases, the majority will recognize its error and reverse its prior action.

The Right of Petition refers to the right of any personally aggrieved member to seek redress within the service structure. Sometimes this right is misunderstood. It does not mean that a group member has the right to apply to the General Service Board or the Conference to reverse a decision taken by a group. In D.A., the groups are at the top of the inverted service triangle; the GSB and the WSC have no power to discipline or correct a group for its actions. Tradition Four, with its emphasis on group autonomy, states this principle forcefully.

Instead, the right applies to situations in which a member of a group is seeking redress within that body. Thus if the Chair of a business meeting arbitrarily refuses to recognize a member who wishes to speak, that member may turn to the whole group for relief by exercising the Right of Petition. A similar right exists if the Chair of a meeting improperly attempts to exclude or silence a member. When a member believes that a group has acted in violation of the Traditions, she or he has the right to seek to change the group's decision at a later meeting.   (In these situations, it should be noted that, while no member may petition the GSB or Conference to reverse a group decision, an aggrieved member may request that the Conference issue a broad statement of policy clarifying the underlying issue for the guidance of all groups in their activities.)

Since the WSC, its committees, the General Service Board, and the GSO are part of the WSC service framework, the Right of Petition may be exercised within this structure. Thus, if an individual GSR or WSC committee believes that a Trustee or Board committee has acted inappropriately, they may petition the Board for redress of grievances. The Board has adopted a process for resolution of these grievances. Ultimately, if an individual has a grievance against the entire GSB, that person may petition a committee of the Conference to bring a motion to direct the Board to reverse its action. Assuming that there is no infringement of the GSB's legal or fiduciary rights, such a motion would be binding upon the Trustees.

Concept 6

The Conference acknowledges the primary administrative responsibility of the Debtors Anonymous General Service Board.

The Conference and its committees have delegated active management of D.A.'s service activities to the General Service Board. While many programs that have been proposed are worthwhile, and some have been successful, for purposes of continuity, these programs should be left to the management and supervision of the General Service Board. The GSB has the legal and fiduciary authority to provide a framework under the GSO to enable these activities to continue, grow, and develop. Where the Board does not have the personnel, time, or money to carry out a particular project, the Conference should recognize that its time has not yet come.

Here, the operative principle is humility. The Conference has recognized, in adopting the Twelve Concepts, that it does not have either the personnel or the expertise to engage in ongoing administrative activities. Whenever it has attempted to do so, difficulties have arisen. The Conference acts through committees, whose memberships change each year. The interests and goals of these members also tend to change and vary. Beyond these practical facts, there lies another spiritual principle. The Third Step suggests that we turn our will and our lives over to the care of our Higher Power. This tells us that we should not use our wills to beat a recalcitrant reality into submission. If time, personnel, or money for a program is not available, we should accept that fact or, if possible, change it by making the time, money, or personnel available through contributions to the GSO in kind, in cash, or by volunteering. We should not rely on ad hoc, under-supported service structures that are all too likely to collapse in order to impose our viewpoints upon the Fellowship.

It is wise to try to couple policy with administration so that both can be effective. When the Conference, acting as the voice and conscience of the Fellowship, makes a decision, it should always try to couch that decision in terms that are broad and flexible, so that the Board, in administering the decision, can develop policies that are effective. In short, those policy choices that are closely tied to administration are best left with those who are to administer them.

Concept 7

The Conference recognizes that the Charter and the Bylaws of the Debtors Anonymous General Service Board serve as governing documents and that the Trustees have legal rights, while the rights of the Conference are spiritual, rooted in the Twelve Traditions. The Concepts are not legal instruments.

The Charter of the Debtors Anonymous General Service Board, Inc. is the legal document used to incorporate the D.A. GSB in the State of New York. It is more commonly called the Articles of Incorporation, and is distinct from the Conference Charter. The general purposes of D.A. as an educational not-for-profit corporation are set forth there. The Bylaws of the Debtors Anonymous General Service Board are more detailed rules covering how our corporate business is conducted under the laws of the State of New York. The bylaws have been adopted by the GSB pursuant to its Articles of Incorporation and are legally binding upon the Board.

These documents stand in contradistinction to the Charter of the D.A. World Service Conference, which has not been filed with any legal entity and does not serve as a legally enforceable document. As a result of its status as a corporation created under the laws of New York State, the General Service Board is the entity legally responsible for carrying out the business affairs of D.A. All property owned by D.A. is legally vested in the Board, and the Board has a fiduciary duty to carry out its responsibilities on behalf of D.A. These are legally binding rights and duties under the laws of New York, and the Board must comply at all times with that jurisdiction's rules, as well as with the rules of any other jurisdiction within which it operates.

Although it does not have any legal significance, the Conference Charter carries great weight within the service structure of D.A. as a whole. It creates and outlines the duties of the World Service Conference, and sets up the structure whereby the GSB is advised and guided in its actions. Because the Conference represents the collective conscience of all of the D.A. groups in the world, it is apparent that the General Service Office and the Board must ordinarily act with the guidance, support, and general approval of the Conference.

However, as noted in the discussion of Concept Two above, the Board has the right to refuse to follow this guidance in cases where there is an infringement of the legal or fiduciary rights of the Trustees. Thus, the Board has refused to act upon a Conference motion which it concluded was in violation of several Traditions in suggesting that groups might in some cases sell and display outside literature. This right to "veto" WSC actions should be exercised only in the most limited and extreme circumstances. For example, if the Conference directed the Board to enter into a lease beyond the ability of the Fellowship to support it without the possibility of future debting, the Trustees might appropriately refuse to do so. This would be true even if no debting were involved, but the future ability of the Fellowship to carry its message would be impaired.

It is the Conference that carries the spiritual force of the group conscience of D.A., and it is the means by which the heart and soul of the Fellowship—the groups and Intergroups—make certain their will is heard. The Conference is given the power under the GSB Bylaws to ratify the appointment of all Trustees, and as noted in connection with Concept Two, the Conference also holds the ultimate power of the purse, which can be used to control the activities of the Trustees. If the Conference were to decide to withhold group and individual contributions from the GSB and GSO, those entities could no longer exist.

Although the Conference Charter is not a legally binding document, the Board has accepted it as the morally binding expression of the will of the groups as to how D.A.'s business is to be conducted. Under Article 4 of the Conference Charter:

"It will be further understood regardless of the legal prerogatives of the General Service Board, as a matter of tradition, that a three-quarter (3/4) vote of all Conference members present may bring about a reorganization of the General Service Board and staff members of the General Service Office, if or when such reorganization is deemed essential."

Here the Board has accepted the ultimate authority of the Conference in the unlikely situation that the Board has seriously disregarded the moral authority of the Conference. Each Board member is bound by an oath (or affirmation) of office to respect and abide by this provision. In fact, this provision is given legal effect by the voluntary action of the Trustees in adopting Article 3.7 of the Bylaws, which provides in part:

> "Class A and Class B Trustees, are expected, subject only to the laws of the State of New York and to these bylaws, at the request of the Conference of Debtors Anonymous, according to the provisions of the D.A. Charter, (that a three-quarter (3/4) vote of all Conference members present may bring about a reorganization of the General Service Board) to resign their trusteeships even though their terms of office as member Trustees may not have expired."

These carefully limited rights and grants of authority interact to produce a thoughtful balance between power and responsibility. When all is said and done, the ultimate authority of the Conference over the Board, as both a practical and spiritual matter, is apparent, but the Board's legal and fiduciary rights are preserved.

Concept 8

The Debtors Anonymous General Service Board of Trustees assumes primary leadership for larger matters of overall policy, finance, and custodial oversight, and delegates authority for routine management of the General Service Office.

Concept Eight recognizes, like Concept Six does, that the realities and practicalities of life require that the GSB take on the role of primary leadership for matters of overall policy. The GSB meets in person and by telephone conference throughout the year. It is a continuing body and has the experience and knowledge necessary to give a broad perspective. The Conference meets for only one short period each year, and its membership changes significantly from year to year—and within the year—as GSR or ISR terms expire and new successors are selected. Although Conference committees meet throughout the year, each has a narrow and limited perspective. For example, the Public Information Committee focuses solely upon matters relating to public information and cooperation with the professional community. The Hospitals, Institutions and Prisons Committee focuses solely upon matters pertaining to these topics. Neither will consider the question of content of literature, which falls to the Literature Committee. What may be desirable for PI may be impossible for HIP. It is the Board which has an overview of all of these activities. The following point should be emphasized here: No committee is the Conference and no committee can act on behalf of the Conference as a whole without specific and carefully limited authorization. Only the GSB has been given the right by the Conference Charter to act as a custodian for D.A. as a whole. Any other result would lead to fragmentation.

Moreover, every organization, even those with the least possible structure, like D.A., requires some point at which a final decision can be made and direction can be provided. Any other approach would result ultimately in the demise of the organization. While the Conference can serve as a guide, advisor, and counselor, it cannot serve as a "hands on" director. The Conference may call the GSB to account, and may, on occasion, overrule the GSB, but it cannot engage in active and ongoing operations.

Here the spiritual concept that is in play is that of self-restraint in all things. In exercising its primary leadership role, the GSB must always bear in mind the Second and Ninth Traditions. The Board must accept that is composed of servants, not masters. D.A. does not operate like other corporate entities. We do not have the typical "top down" structure; ordinarily, we do not pass on orders and directives from "the top." Instead, we strive to apply the Steps, Traditions, and Concepts in all of our operations; we attempt to reason and to persuade. Concepts Three, Four, and Five should always influence our thoughts and actions. The Board should accept the fact that its decisions may and should be questioned and challenged. And the Board should always be accountable and be prepared to explain its actions. Most importantly, the Board must always be willing to admit error, if error there be, and strive to correct that error immediately.

Concept Eight also ties directly into Concept Seven. Because the Board has legal rights and duties, it is the only entity in the service structure which can appropriately handle the finances and properties necessary to fulfilling our publishing and other educational functions. Thus, matters of finance and custodial oversight of property are entrusted to the Board. Again, these powers should always be read against the background of the Steps, Traditions, and Concepts. Just like the Conference, the GSB should never become "the seat of perilous wealth or power." The principle of corporate poverty—accumulating only what is necessary to carry out our functions—should be our guide.

Within this context, certain ideas unique to Twelve Step programs are, however, important. Unlike the ordinary employer, the GSB is bound by the Third Concept. We must always strive to avoid micromanagement of the activities of the Office. While the Office is there to assist the Board and D.A. as a whole in carrying out its activities, how it routinely performs these functions should be within the discretion of the staff. This is always subject to the caveat that there may be situations in which the routine itself becomes objectionable and harmful to D.A.'s paramount interests; in such instances, the Trustees have both the right and the obligation to intervene. Decisions should not be imposed upon the Office; under the Fourth Concept, the staff should be consulted before a final decision is made. And, the staff should always be permitted to petition the Board for changes in duties and working conditions under Concept Five.

Concept 9

Good leaders, together with appropriate methods for choosing them at all levels, are necessary. At the world service level, the Board of Trustees assumes primary leadership for D.A. as a whole.

Leadership is an important idea for both the Twelve Traditions and the Twelve Concepts. The Second Tradition points out that "our leaders are but trusted servants; they do not govern." This Concept points out the need for good leadership in D.A. But what, precisely, is it?

It is clear that leadership in D.A. is not the same as leadership in the corporate or political worlds. There, leadership takes on an aura of governance. That type of good leader is one who directs or governs well. However, in D.A., the idea of servant leadership is the prevailing approach. This means that the GSB, in exercising its leadership role, must always be aware of the limits of its authority.

First of all, leaders in D.A. must recognize that they exercise only a delegated authority. The right of the Trustees to act on behalf of D.A. stems from the fact that the groups and their delegates have recognized their right to do so. The leaders in D.A. are those who can generate respect and acceptance for their actions because they are understood to be acting for the good of D.A. as a whole. This requires that the Board and GSO listen carefully to the D.A. groups as they express themselves in the conscience of the Conference. It is essential that leaders be open to persuasion and discourse. This also applies to group and Intergroup officers and representatives.

This is not to say that good leaders always necessarily follow what they perceive to be the "popular" route. In many instances, the welfare of the whole requires that unpopular actions be taken, and good leaders must be willing to do so when necessary. This leads to a second requirement of good leadership. A leader in D.A. must always be willing to explain their actions. Here, clarity and precision are important. Leaders must be sure to think things through and formulate clear and convincing justifications for their contemplated actions. Also, a good leader must be able and willing to lead through persuasion. A calm and reasoned approach will be effective in helping to explain conduct that, at first blush, may be unpopular.

Another element of good leadership is prudence. We must always recognize that our actions in D.A.

service have consequences. Those consequences may be serious, whether on the group level or the World Service level. The good leader does not "shoot from the hip" or act on the spur of the moment. Thought and care are important elements of any decision. We should always remember that when we act in service we are acting on behalf of a Fellowship that has saved our lives and that will continue to save the lives of others if we act prudently. Rash or impulsive conduct in service is always inappropriate. Just as our personal stories often illustrate that a misplaced sense of urgency can lead to debting, so too can a false urgency result in poor leadership.

Humility is at least as important as prudence. The leaders in a Twelve Step Fellowship must always be willing to recognize and accept their limitations as well as those of others. In service it is all too easy to become self-righteous and insistent upon the need to do things in only one way. This mind frame must be avoided at all costs. The good leader must always be willing to admit error and seek better ways of doing things. Closely allied with this is a sense of humor. The ability to laugh at ourselves is central to good leadership. We must be careful not to take ourselves too seriously, and we must always be ready to place our conduct in the perspective of humor. Beyond this, the ability to laugh and to see the lighter side is helpful in ensuring that we do not become bogged down in our own narrow view of things.

Charity is not only a virtue; it is an essential element of leadership. The ability to reach out and seek to understand and support those around us makes the tasks of all easier. The desire to forgive perceived slights and to move on in unity is of inestimable value. If our service is not motivated by a love of our fellows and a desire to help and assist, it is a vain and empty gesture. Twelfth Step work, at whatever level of service, always proceeds from the impulse of love for our fellows.

Finally, two of the most important elements in leadership are faith and hope. Leaders must have faith in their Higher Power and in the Fellowship of D.A. They must always be willing to strive for the highest good for D.A. Hope leads us on in service to achieve great goals for the Fellowship and for our fellows. Hope convinces us that we can be better and that we can do better.

This sounds like an almost impossible list of attributes for any one person to have. In fact, it may be. Few, if any, among us have all of these qualifications in full measure. But many of us have these attributes to some degree. Some have one or more in great degree. And, when we work together, the full body will have all of these gifts. Our strength is in our unity.

How do we develop and discover these attributes? This is perhaps the hardest question. Sometimes the person possessing these abilities is quiet and these qualities may be obscured by reticence. However, in our groups we come to know each other remarkably well. After all, we have gone through a life-changing experience together in joining D.A. and in working its program. The still, quiet voice often becomes apparent as the voice of wisdom if we listen and continue to love each other. As we grow through working the Twelve Steps, these qualities become increasingly apparent. Experience leads to strength and hope.

Concept 10

Every D.A. service responsibility should be equal to its service authority as defined by tradition, resolution, or D.A.'s Charter.

The Tenth Concept states a simple but vital fact: in delegating authority, it is always important to define the scope of that authority clearly and to grant whatever powers may be necessary to carry out this responsibility. This Concept is closely allied with, and flows naturally from, Concept Three. The "Right of Decision" in that Concept provides the means for carrying out the intent of Concept Ten. If we give an individual the responsibility to do something, we must also give that person the necessary authority to accomplish that end. The delegating authority, whether it be the groups, the Conference or the Board, must be careful to relinquish day-to-day control and recognize the right of the recipient of that authority to act as their conscience and knowledge may dictate. It should be noted that this Concept states an ideal. When one is dealing with words, there is almost no way to ensure an absence of ambiguity in both foreseeable and unforeseeable cases. In some cases, ambiguity will develop, no matter how much thought has gone into the words. In such cases, honest efforts must be made to resolve these ambiguities, in light of tradition, the Steps, the Traditions, and other contexts.

Every effort should be made to ensure that the nature and limits of that authority are clearly set forth. Sometimes authority exists from before the time of any grant. Thus, the GSB preexisted the writing of the Charter, and much of the Board's authority is defined by tradition that developed in the years before the Conference was created. Here, the Bylaws of the GSB and its Articles of Incorporation (Charter) may contain limitations upon its activities. And again, the Twelve Traditions in D.A. may spell out the limitations on authority. It is clear that all groups are bound by the Fourth Tradition not to engage in conduct that may be harmful to other groups or to D.A. as a whole. It is equally clear that the GSB is bound by the Seventh Tradition's prohibition of outside contributions, and that the Conference is bound by the Tenth Tradition's admonition to avoid "public controversy."

When the Conference creates a new committee, a mission statement is adopted defining the scope of that committee's activities. It is important that no committee exceed its authority or impinge on the duties of any other committee. For example, Conference-approved literature begins with the Literature Committee. While some other committee may request that the Literature Committee consider approving the concept of a particular piece of literature, no other committee should be engaged in writing and/or editing literature.

The GSB delegates authority to run the routine operations of the GSO to the Office Manager. However, the Board retains a supervisory, policy-making and leadership role in all of the activities of the GSO. At times, it is difficult to define the limits of these two different types of authority. In such cases, there must be an effort made to ensure that there is no overreaching. Where there is doubt, efforts must be made to seek clarity. It is obvious, however, that the Board must remain the final authority with respect to actions taken, since it is legally responsible for all GSO activities.

Concept 11

While the Trustees hold final authority for D.A. World Service administration, they will be assisted by the best possible staff members and consultants. Therefore, serious care and consideration will always be given to the compensation, selection, induction to service, rotation, and assignments for special rights and duties for all staff with a proper basis for determining financial compensation.

The status, selection, and pay of staff and consultants are the subjects of this Concept. Most important is the injunction that the GSB exercise serious care and consideration in using its authority in this area.

As a small Fellowship, D.A. does not have a large staff. At this writing, there is one full-time Office Manager and one part-time staff assistant. In the past, care has been taken in selecting the Manager, and their selection of an assistant has been done in consultation with the GSB. This procedure should continue; if another full-time employee is hired, it is to be expected that the Board would have similar input into their selection. While matters of general policy remain with the Trustees, the means by which these policies and goals are attained have been left to the initial discretion of the Manager, subject to general policy. The Board oversees the Office and its employees through an Office Committee, which includes an Office Liaison who regularly communicates with the Office Manager. An annual review of the work of the Office Manager is undertaken by the Office Liaison, and this is reported to the Office Committee and the full Board.

The Board gives great attention to the matter of compensation. Again, as a small Fellowship, we must pay close attention to finances. However, this does not mean that we are miserly. The Trustees have an obligation to hire the best possible staff, and this means that our wages must be competitive to ensure that we hire and retain experienced and capable employees. Each year the Office Committee of the Board undertakes a review of the full-time salary of the Office Manager as well as the benefits that are provided. The Office Committee, in conjunction with the Finance Committee, takes great care and deliberation in this area, and the full Board reviews and approves any final decision as to compensation.

This Concept also deals with the relation of the General Service Board to the General Service Office. Here, the principle of "custodial oversight" must be balanced against the idea of delegation of "routine management." From the start, it should be clear that the relation between the GSB and the staff of the GSO is, ultimately, the relation of employer to employee. Employee professionalism and dedication are underlying principles of that relationship, just like respect, fairness, and honesty on the part of the Board. The World Service Conference is not a direct participant in this relationship. That authority has been delegated by the groups to the Trustees. Without a clear understanding of this principle, we would be entering the dangerous fields of double-headed management. While the Conference or a committee may advise, it should never interfere.

The Board has employed outside consultants most often in the areas of legal and technology/Internet services. We also employ outside assistance in the editorial preparation, layout, translation, and publication of our literature and some reports. We have sometimes been fortunate in finding members of the Board who have been generous with their services in these areas, providing free assistance. When outsiders are chosen, efforts are made to ensure that their rates are competitive and that they will perform competently. In small matters, the Board will dispense with competitive bids, particularly where speed is of the essence, but in any large-scale employment, such as the contract for writing the Twelve Steps and Twelve Traditions book, requests for proposals are used. In all non-bidding situations, the committee supervising the activity usually has a clear understanding of what rates are competitive.

This Concept on its face applies only to staff and consultants hired by the Trustees. However, it provides a model for the groups and Intergroups as well, in selecting their officers and committees. Thus, great care should be exercised in the selection of a treasurer. Prudent supervision of our finances must always be our goal in Debtors Anonymous. Experience and recovery are important qualifications in this area. The position of GSR or ISR should also be given careful consideration. When a person is selected to fill one of those positions, she or he will be making decisions that may affect the future of D.A. for years to come. We should give at least as much care to the selection of such people as we would give to the selection of those who are to care for our children. After all, D.A. is the future of all of us.

Concept 12

The Conference of Debtors Anonymous will observe the spirit of the Traditions, taking care not to become powerful and wealthy; having sufficient operating funds with a prudent reserve; having no authority over any other members; making important decisions by discussing and voting on issues wherever possible by substantial unanimity; not acting in a punitive way; not inciting public controversy; never performing any acts of government; and finally, always remaining democratic in thought and action.

Concept Twelve contains what are called the "General Warranties" of the Conference. Similar language is contained in Article 10 of the Conference Charter, and may be changed only with the consent of three-quarters of the registered groups in D.A. Since this is the same requirement for amending the Twelve Steps and the Twelve Traditions, it is obvious how important these Warranties were to those who founded the Fellowship of Debtors Anonymous.

Each of these Warranties is related to fundamental ideas in our spiritual program of recovery.

"taking care not to become powerful and wealthy"

Here, the Second and Seventh Traditions are best recalled. We are reminded again of the humbling fact that our leaders are only trusted servants. They do not govern. They have no power to discipline or expel. Instead, they operate on the basis of their honest understanding of what the will of the Higher Power is for D.A., putting aside personal goals, ambitions, and resentments. Just as the GSB is bound by the ideal of corporate poverty, so is the Conference.

"having sufficient operating funds with a prudent reserve"

The Second Warranty is one that goes to the heart of the D.A. recovery program. Careful supervision of our finances is a duty of the Conference, just as it is an individual responsibility for all members as well as the Trustees of the General Service Board. We are to put into practice on the service level what we have learned on the recovery level.

"having no authority over any other members"

The Third Warranty stands in stark contrast to corporate or political models of social organization. The Conference has no power to direct the recovery of any individual. While it may put forward suggestions and share with the Board the experience, strength, and hope of D.A. members over the decades, it may not mandate a course of conduct, either in recovery or in other parts of our lives. How each member achieves their spiritual life is a matter of individual conscience. The Conference, unlike a church or other spiritual body, has no right to attempt to direct that conscience.

"making important decisions by discussing and voting on issues wherever possible by substantial unanimity"

The Fourth Warranty's requirements of discussion and substantial unanimity ensure that D.A.'s Conference will act thoughtfully and prudently. This ties in with the Rights of Appeal and Petition of the Fifth Concept. The Conference must always make an effort to listen to and consider the minority voice. Deliberations should not be hasty; we should always be willing to reconsider in matters of importance. When actions are taken, they should reflect the clear will of the membership; a mere majority should not be able to impose its will on a substantial minority. Thus, a two-thirds vote has, in practice, been required for most major decisions of the Conference.

"not acting in a punitive way"

The requirement of Warranty Five reinforces the idea that the Conference does not exercise authority over the membership of D.A. There is no enforcement mechanism in D.A. to allow the Conference to impose its will upon members. There is no right of censure or expulsion, no excommunication or denial of membership. The Conference reflects the voice and the conscience of D.A. as a whole. That is the source of whatever authority it might have in a moral sense. It has none in a worldly sense. Like all of the other Warranties, this should also apply at the group and Intergroup levels. There should be no room for punishment in D.A. Love and service should be our motto.

"not inciting public controversy"

The Sixth Warranty is closely related to the Tenth Tradition. As a group, D.A. has no opinion on outside issues; we should always refrain from conduct that might appear to be an endorsement or support of anything outside our primary purpose. This does not mean that the Conference should not debate issues that properly come before it. Disagreement is the anvil on which truth is forged. We must always be willing to assert our honestly held opinions when this will further the good of D.A.; it is never appropriate to involve D.A. in controversy on outside issues.

"never performing any acts of government"

Under the Seventh Warranty, the Conference, including the General Service Board, should never perform acts of government. It should not seek to bind the membership to any belief system or code of conduct. It should recognize the importance of the individual in D.A. And it should accept that differences in approach and opinion will always exist in a free society.

"always remaining democratic in thought and action."

Finally, the Eighth Warranty is a guarantee that D.A. will always adhere to democratic principles in conducting its business. If we adhere to the other Concepts, the Steps, and the Traditions, this should pose no problem. Throughout its history, D.A. has emphasized the right of individual conscience and the rights of individuals. Democracy implies this and more. It implies a corresponding duty on the part of the minority to accept the majority decision as the will of the Higher Power. There should be no efforts to undermine, or walking away in anger. If a mistake has been made, it will eventually become apparent to most. At that time, and only then, should efforts be made to change the decision of the majority reached by substantial unanimity.

The Twelve Concepts for Debtors Anonymous were inspired by the Twelve Concepts for Alcoholics Anonymous and are modified with permission of A.A. World Services, Inc.

Addendum: A Glossary of Acronyms and Service Terms Commonly Used in Debtors Anonymous

UNFORTUNATE BUT NECESSARY DISCLAIMER: The definitions and descriptions offered herein are not the opinion of the Debtors Anonymous General Service Board, Inc., or claim to be an exhaustive explanation of the terms, jargon, or acronyms commonly used in D.A. service. Where possible, quotations from D.A. literature are used and noted. Outside sources have been credited where necessary. For further amplification, we recommend reading D.A. Conference-Approved literature.

Updated: July 2020

ACM Appointed Committee Member. "Each committee of the General Service Board may choose to select one or more Appointed Committee Members (ACMs) to serve on the committee. These ACMs are recovering D.A. members who usually have needed experience or expertise in a particular field, such as computer technology, literature development, or public relations." (ACM FAQ, 2009)

ACOH / ACOH2 A Currency of Hope serves as D.A.'s basic text, originally published in 1999. The second edition was released in 2014.

Anonymity One of the D.A. Tools. Tradition Eleven states: "Our public relations policy is based on attraction rather than promotion; we need always maintain personal anonymity at the level of press, radio, and films." Tradition Twelve states: "Anonymity is the spiritual foundation of all our Traditions, ever reminding us to place principles before personalities."

Area Group / GSR Area Group A group of GSRs (General Service Representatives) representing local D.A. groups who come together in a metropolitan area, region, or state to perform and share about local/regional service activities.

BDA Business Debtors Anonymous is a distinct but not separate part of D.A., created to focus on the recovery of members of the fellowship who are business owners. BDA meetings focus on business owner's issues, but are open to all D.A. In the D.A. literature catalog, the pamphlet Business Debtors Anonymous, item P-122, explains the warning signs for debting in business and provides tools for running our businesses. "BDA" also refers to the BDA Committee of the WSC (World Service Conference). The BDA Committee focuses on issues specific to the needs of D.A. members who own or operate businesses, are self-employed, or have a desire to own or operate a business or be self-employed. The BDA Committee is open to all GSRs and ISRs (Intergroup Service Representatives), not just those who represent BDA groups.

Bylaws "The Bylaws of the D.A. General Service Board are a legal document and cannot be suspended even with a unanimous vote, but can usually be amended with a vote of substantial unanimity. The bylaws cannot be in conflict with the Twelve Traditions, the D.A. Conference Charter, or the laws of the State of New York or the United States. . . . The Trustees are subject to the laws of the State of New York, and are expected to exercise the powers vested in them by law in a manner consonant with the faith that permeates and guides the Fellowship, inspired by the Twelve Steps, in accordance with the Traditions, and in keeping with the Certificate and the bylaws." (Debtors Anonymous Manual for Service (DAMS), 2014, p. 118)

Caucus Informal caucuses discuss the concerns of (1) Intergroup, and (2) Spiritually Sustainable Earning, and (3) Underserved and Under-represented Outreach. The caucus is an additional service commitment that any delegate may participate in along with their regular committee assignment. WSC committees can make motions at Convocation while caucuses propose recommendations. Caucuses wishing to bring a motion must do so through a WSC committee.

CC   The Conference Committee of the WSC. The Conference Committee is concerned with the general nature of the World Service Conference. This includes the Charter of the World Service Conference and its relationship to the General Service Board and membership of D.A. as a whole; issues related to the format of the annual World Service Conference of Debtors Anonymous; assistance to the Host Committee in their planning and logistics; and recommendations of sites for future annual conferences.

Charter / Conference Charter   The Conference Charter is the principal document of communication between the GSRs, Intergroups, and the GSB. It outlines the rights and responsibilities of D.A.'s WSC.

Class A   Compulsive debtor Trustees of the D.A. GSB. Class A Trustees are those who have arrested their compulsive debting; have not incurred new, unsecured debt for a period of at least three years; and are living so far as possible within the principles of the Debtors Anonymous Twelve Steps. Current bylaws allow a maximum of ten Class A trustees on the board.

Class B   Non-debtor Trustees of the D.A. GSB. Class B Trustees are those who are not now and have not been afflicted by the disease of compulsive debting and who express a profound faith in the D.A. program. Current bylaws allow a maximum of five (5) Class B trustees on the board.

Committee (GSB and WSC)   The work of the fellowship gets done by the D.A. GSB, by the WSC Committees and Caucuses at the Conference, and over the course of the WSC Conference year. As of 2015, there are ten (10) WSC committees. There are twelve (12) GSB committees. Many, but not all, of the GSB committees have a corresponding WSC counterpart, and vice versa.

Convocation   The voting sessions of the WSC, held over two days, where the annual business of D.A. is addressed. Following the Conference's activities and committee meetings, registered GSRs, ISRs, current GSB trustees, and the GSO office manager are asked to vote on important issues affecting D.A. as a whole, including approval of literature, committee work, and spending plans, and other issues, such as unity, as proposed by the WSC committees and the GSB.

A Currency of Hope   (see ACOH)

DAMS   The Debtors Anonymous Manual for Service was first published in 2011. It supplanted the GSR/ISR Manual with updated contents of that piece along with much new material and twelve essays on the Concepts. It is updated regularly by the GSB Long Range Planning Committee.

Delegate   A voting participant at the WSC, who could be a GSR, an ISR, a trustee, or GSO office manager. Every D.A. group and Intergroup is entitled to send one delegate to the WSC at the group's expense every year.

eNews   One of the many avenues of communication the GSB has established with the fellowship, eNews is distributed to subscribers using a commercial social media platform.

FAQ / Frequently Asked Questions   A compilation of responses that seek to answer readers' common questions on a specific subject. There are several FAQs on the D.A. website: FAQs for newcomers on the homepage of the D.A. website, one about becoming a trustee and another about becoming an ACM. D.A. also includes an FAQ in the Treasurer's Manual.

FCC   Fellowship Communications Committee of the WSC. The Fellowship Communications Committee facilitates communication and promotes collaboration among the debtors who still suffer, the Debtors Anonymous membership, the World Service Conference committees and caucuses, the General Service Office, and the General Service Board.

Fellowship-Wide Call   The GSB Long Range Planning Committee (LRPC) and other WSC Committees and Caucuses host conference calls on a variety of subjects. These are announced well in advance of the event, and recordings of the presentation are available as podcasts on the D.A. website to the fellowship for those who could not attend.

Focus / the DA Focus   The DA Focus is the GSB's quarterly report to the Fellowship of D.A., reflecting the activities of the D.A. General Service Board and World Service Conference. It includes details on service-related occurrences, primarily at the World Service level, updates throughout the year on the work of GSB and WSC committees, and financial reports for D.A. as a whole.

General Service Representative (GSR)   A registered local D.A. group's elected representative, who acts as the primary link between the group and the Fellowship as a whole. The GSR assumes responsibility of performing service for the WSC of D.A. and may serve for up to two consecutive three-year terms. At the Conference, GSRs serve as Delegates.

GSB   General Service Board of Trustees, Inc., is responsible for putting into practice D.A.'s group conscience as expressed through the will of the World Service Conference. The Board also fulfills all fiduciary responsibilities required by law of nonprofit corporations; the Trustees perform serious legally-imposed duties, such as protecting copyrights and trademarks and filing required forms and tax returns. The General Service Office (GSO) assists the GSB in carrying out these responsibilities. The Trustees may serve for up to two three-year terms.

GSO   The General Service Office, presently based in Needham, MA, is the administrative "heart" of Debtors Anonymous, carrying out D.A.'s primary purpose—to carry the message to the still-suffering compulsive debtor—every day. It is the hub of day-to-day communication with the suffering newcomer, with D.A. members and groups and Intergroups, between the groups and the General Service Board, with the media, and with the larger world. Special workers, acting within the D.A. Traditions and guided by the D.A. Concepts of Service, serve a growing number of groups and members around the world.

HIP   The Hospitals, Institutions, and Prisons Committee is composed of GSRs and ISRs who would like to focus service efforts on carrying the message of D.A. to debtors confined in hospitals, institutions, and prisons.

Host (Committee)   Since the WSC rotates around the United States from year to year, a local "host" committee performs much of the "boots on the ground" work of planning and executing the Conference.

Intergroup   The Intergroup is a local or regional organization that supports, and is supported by, the area D.A. groups. The Intergroup provides services for newcomers, members, and groups, which may include a hotline/voicemail, area meeting lists, a website, and sponsoring special events. Together we can accomplish what none of us could accomplish separately. This is the simple principle underlying the need for Intergroups. The primary purpose of any group is to carry the message of recovery to the still-suffering debtor. In many instances, a group operating by itself cannot do this effectively. Thus, a group of ten or twelve members would find it both expensive and difficult to undertake creation of a 'hot line', or even a telephone line and answering machine, for inquiries by potential members. One group might not be able to take advantage of quantity discounts in buying literature from the GSO. These activities, so important in carrying the message, can be facilitated through creation of an Intergroup. Beyond this basic and fundamental purpose, an Intergroup can serve as a clearinghouse for information. Groups can send representatives to general meetings of an Intergroup and share their experience, strength, and hope in carrying the message. New ideas and approaches can be exchanged. Groups can learn what is happening elsewhere in their area and share their knowledge and experience with new or struggling groups.

Intergroup (Caucus)   The Intergroup Caucus is composed primarily of ISRs but also includes GSRs who have experience with their local Intergroups. The main function of this caucus is to create tools, resources, and a better understanding of the role of an Intergroup in the overall organizational structure of D.A. The Intergroup Caucus helps support both new and existing Intergroups. The Intergroup Caucus also contributes to the efforts to regionalize D.A.

Intergroup Service Representative (ISR)   a registered local or area D.A. Intergroup representative elected or appointed (the Intergroup's decision) who assumes responsibility of acting as a liaison between the WSC and the Intergroup and who performs service for the World Service Conference. The ISR may serve for up to two consecutive three-year terms.

International Committee (INT)   The International Caucus became the International Committee at the 2019 WSC. The International Committees' mission is to exchange information and develop initiatives to support the growth of D.A. internationally.

IOC   Internal Operations Committee of the WSC. The primary responsibility of the Internal Operations Committee (IOC) is to support the General Service Office (GSO) of Debtors Anonymous. The committee (1) focuses on the overall office operations of the General Service Office, and (2) interacts with the Board Office Liaison and the Office Manager to support the ongoing work of the GSO.

John H.   The idea that would give rise to the Fellowship of Debtors Anonymous started in 1968, when a core group of recovering members of Alcoholics Anonymous® began discussing the problems they were experiencing with money. Led by a man named John H., they began an eight-year spiritual odyssey to understand the causes and conditions behind their self-destructive behavior with money.

John H. Scholarship Fund   A reserve fund earmarked to provide support for delegates traveling to the WSC. Members and groups are encouraged to contribute to the fund, which benefits under-supported groups.

Liaison   Every WSC committee and caucus is assigned a trustee yearly to facilitate communication between the WSC entity and the GSB. Each trustee receives a liaison assignment from the GSB Chairperson following their ratification as a new trustee.

LITCOM   Literature Committee of the WSC. D.A. conference-approved literature begins with the Literature Committee. Members participate in all levels of the literature creative process, including generating ideas for new D.A. literature, working closely with members of Literature Publications, reviewing drafts of literature in process (given to them at the Conference by Literature Publications), approving final drafts of D.A. literature, and bringing motions to approve drafts of literature to Convocation to become conference-approved literature.

MCP   Media Contact Person, someone who has undergone media contact training and is prepared to meet with press or media to provide accurate information about D.A. within the context of the Twelve Traditions.

MCT   Media contact training prepares D.A. members to meet with press or media to provide accurate information about D.A. within the context of the Twelve Traditions.

Modified Forum   A shorter, often half-day version of a Regional Forum. Modified Forums are sometimes offered to the local Intergroup, if any, during the GSB's winter Face-to-Face meeting.

PI COM / WSC PI   Public Information Committee of the WSC. The Public Information Committee interfaces with the media, helping professionals, and the general public in person, on the telephone, and through written information.

PIR   Public Information Representative. We seek to be a credible community resource by providing information on D.A. websites and via other communications to the general public, the media, and helping professionals. We also provide information to institutions when there is no local Hospitals, Institutions, and Prisons (HIP) committee. PIRs report to their Intergroup or home group meeting.

Project Contributor (PC) An opportunity for a member to participate in service to a GSB Committee on a specific task or project, generally for a term of approximately 3-9 months. Former D.A. trustees are eligible to apply to serve as Project Contributors one year following completion of their GSB service.

Prudent Reserve   A term that originates in Concept 12, a prudent reserve is a financial cushion for a D.A. group, or Intergroup, and the GSB, which could help the group weather a short –term or long-term decrease in revenue.

RDC Resource Development Committee of the WSC. Revenue for D.A. is the focus of the Resource Development Committee, including (1) increasing Seventh Tradition contributions and clarifying the use of Seventh Tradition funds, (2) encouraging member participation in service at all levels, and (3) increasing awareness within the D.A. Fellowship about the importance of self-support.

Region Regions can refer to Intergroup regions, Regional Area Group regions, or Regional Intergroups. Developing a process for defining regions is a current undertaking at the D.A. World Level. Previously "Regions," in Section 3.5 in the Bylaws, referred to the number of Class A trustees that could serve on the GSB from a particular geographic location. In 2020, regional limits for Class A Trustees were eliminated.

Regional Forum The purpose of a Regional Forum is to help develop a culture of service within D.A. This is accomplished by working in tandem with a local Intergroup to present a day-long workshop for members of D.A. focusing in on a number of issues. Among the issues discussed are the work and finances of the General Service Board (GSB), the process by which D.A. literature is developed, the General Service Office (GSO), the history of D.A., and the D.A. Archives. In addition, Intergroup participants present a discussion of opportunities for service on the Intergroup level and all participants share in a discussion of the importance of the Twelve Traditions to personal recovery. Forums present an opportunity for D.A. members to interact with members of the GSB and to seek answers to questions they may have. They also provide a chance for members of D.A. to present suggestions to the GSB and to interact with Board members in formulating future goals for D.A. In addition, they give the Board members an occasion to meet with individual members and Intergroup officers and representatives to learn more of the problems and difficulties facing each part of the Fellowship.

RFP / Request for Proposal A document posted by an organization to elicit bids from potential vendors for a product or service. The RFP clearly delineates the deliverables that will be required.

Rotation The idea of rotation of service positions is one of long standing in Twelve Step fellowships. It traces its origin to the original, "long form" version of the Twelve Traditions, as originally printed by Alcoholics Anonymous® in 1946. . . . The cofounder of A.A., Bill W., also referred to the idea of rotation in A.A.'s Concept XII. . . . D.A. members, like those of other programs, are often ego-driven personalities. We tend to seek to dominate and control, either overtly or covertly. There is a strong drive to seek to politicize and manipulate. While these tendencies can lead to progress and positive change, they can also lead to rigidity and inflexibility. At the extreme, they can lead to division and hostility as those who are dominated or manipulated realize what is happening. Ultimately, these tendencies are anti-democratic in nature and can work to undermine the effectiveness of the D.A. Program.

Service Material Service Material is produced in response to the needs of D.A. members for information and shared experience on specific service-related subjects. It reflects the guidance of the Twelve Traditions, the General Service Board (GSB) and the General Service Office (GSO), and is developed from the shared experience of D.A. members throughout the Fellowship. Since Service Material reflects the current and ever-developing conscience of our Fellowship as a whole, it does not undergo the usual D.A. literature approval process, requiring final approval by the World Service Conference (WSC), and may be updated periodically under the auspices of the General Service Board to reflect current Fellowship experience.

Service Sponsor Someone who has strong background in the service structure; practices the Twelve Steps, Twelve Traditions, Twelve Concepts, and is willing to share their experience, strength and hope in the different aspects of service.

Special Worker Special workers are referenced in Tradition Eight: "D.A. should remain forever nonprofessional, but our service centers may employ special workers." Although D.A. is an all-volunteer organization in terms of active Twelfth-Step work, Intergroups and GSO may hire paid employees to ensure continuity and coverage of vital services.

Spiritually Sustainable Earning (Caucus) The Spiritually Sustainable Earning Caucus (SSEC) serves to support the D.A. Fellowship in gaining clarity around issues of earning in the D.A. program. Our vision is to broaden the fellowship-wide understanding of how spiritually sustainable earning fits into D.A. recovery, encouraging a comprehensive and spiritual approach by working the Twelve Steps and using the Tools of Debtors Anonymous.

Sponsor-A-Group is modeled after individual sponsorship to help connect strong and well-resourced groups with groups that are either just getting started or are in need of additional guidance and support. This group-to-group sponsorship exists between two D.A. meetings: A D.A. Sponsor Group and a D.A. Sponsee Group.

Style Guide In an effort to standardize grammatical usage, punctuation, capitalization, and use of the D.A. trademark, the GSB Communication Committee has written and maintains a "D.A. Style Guide," which offers our paid writers and editors, as well as committee members, stylistic standards for D.A. written and electronic communications.

Substantial Unanimity As used in the D.A. GSB bylaws, substantial unanimity means a two-thirds majority of the current trustees voting.

Tech / TECHCOM Technology Committee of the WSC. The Technology Committee is composed of delegates who have experience with and/or interest in leveraging technology to grow D.A. The Tech Committee focuses on harnessing technology to improve access to D.A.'s resources, facilitate communication within D.A., and reach out to the debtor who still suffers. The committee advises the Conference and the GSB, as well as providing hands-on technical expertise where applicable.

Underserved and Under-represented Outreach (Committee) The mission of the Underserved and Under-represented Outreach Committee is to support the Fellowship in carrying the message of Debtors Anonymous to the debtor in underserved populations and locations. We coordinate with World Service Conference committees and caucuses by developing best practices for doing that work and sharing it with D.A. as a whole.

Warranties In all its proceedings, the General Service Conference shall observe the spirit of Debtors Anonymous Traditions, taking great care that the Conference never becomes the seat of perilous wealth or power; that sufficient operating funds, plus an ample reserve, be its prudent financial principle; that none of the Conference members shall ever be placed in a position of unqualified authority over any of the others; that all important decisions be reached by discussion, vote, and whenever possible by substantial unanimity; that no Conference action ever be personally punitive or an incitement to public controversy; that though the Conference may act for the service of Debtors Anonymous, it shall never perform any acts of government; and that, like the Society of Debtors Anonymous which it serves, the Conference itself will always remain democratic in thought and action.

Ways & Means® An electronic meeting in print for the Fellowship of Debtors Anonymous, [*Ways & Means*] is published quarterly by the D.A. General Service Board, and is posted on the D.A. website, www.debtorsanonymous.org. It is a forum for sharing the experience, strength, and hope of D.A. members, groups, and other service bodies. Articles represent the viewpoints of their authors, and are not intended to be statements of D.A. policy.

World Service Conference (WSC) This is the Annual Business Meeting of Debtors Anonymous, where matters affecting the fellowship as a whole are addressed. The WSC is the guardian of D.A. world services and the Twelve Steps and Twelve Traditions of Debtors Anonymous.

World Service Month April is designated as World Service Month to commemorate the (traditional) anniversary date of the founding of D.A., April 15, 1976, by reminding members to practice the Seventh Tradition.

(Have a suggestion for another glossary term? Contact the GSO at office@debtorsanonymous. org.)

Printed in Great Britain
by Amazon

83640655R00086